THE CREATIVE LEARNING TOOLKIT

The Creative Learning Toolkit provides primary educators with inclusive activities that support learning through creative exploration. Each activity is crafted to ensure that children of all abilities can participate and thrive, with step-by-step instructions accompanied by insightful tips on adapting activities to different learning needs.

The book includes an array of hands-on-projects, thoughtfully curated to enhance communication, motor skills, and more, from imaginative art projects that encourage self-expression to science experiments that ignite curiosity. Each chapter focusses on an area that will achieve creativity and provide progression through the curriculum, with ideas, plans, differentiation, and extensions offering activities that provide a solid basis to lessons and can be used flexibly as starters, finishers, or full lessons.

With a wealth of illustrations to bring each activity to life, this book is a valuable resource for primary school teachers, teaching assistants, and SENCOs looking to support and enrich the curriculum with creative activities for all.

Kerry Thalia is the Founding Director of Discover Inclusion and has experience working in mainstream and alternative provision schools with children with a range of needs. She has worked with children all over the world, from the Arctic Circle to Costa Rica. Her enthusiasm for inclusion for all, along with her own neurodivergence, drove her to set up Discover Inclusion.

THE CREATIVE LEARNING TOOLKIT

INCLUSIVE AND ACCESSIBLE ACTIVITIES FOR THE PRIMARY CLASSROOM

Kerry Thalia

Routledge
Taylor & Francis Group
LONDON AND NEW YORK

Designed cover image: Kerry Thalia

First published 2025
by Routledge
4 Park Square, Milton Park, Abingdon, Oxon OX14 4RN

and by Routledge
605 Third Avenue, New York, NY 10158

Routledge is an imprint of the Taylor & Francis Group, an informa business

British Library Cataloguing-in-Publication Data
A catalogue record for this book is available from the British Library

ISBN: 978-1-032-84834-1 (hbk)
ISBN: 978-1-032-84833-4 (pbk)
ISBN: 978-1-003-51523-4 (ebk)

DOI: 10.4324/9781003515234

Typeset in DIN Pro
by Deanta Global Publishing Services, Chennai, India

Ben, thank you for your never-ending support.

CONTENTS

ACKNOWLEDGEMENTS

I'm extremely grateful to Ann Sullivan for her invaluable patience and feedback, and for supporting me in writing despite the difficulties of dyslexia. Over the past couple of years, Ann has taught me a lot about phonics for SEND children, which is reflected in the "Phonics" chapter.

This book would also not have been possible without Emma Alsayedahmad and her moral support during the illustration process, which kept me moving forward and enjoying those already completed.

Lastly, I'd like to mention the writing completed by my cat, Muffin, ensuring that I read over the entire manuscript before submission in case of any impromptu dksjlg.

INTRODUCTION

As parents, educators, and caregivers, we recognise the power of fostering a supportive and enriching learning environment for our children. We understand the significance of imparting knowledge while nurturing their innate curiosity and creativity. This book is the culmination of those aspirations – a guide designed to bridge the gap between learning and fun, all within the reach of the classroom. It is a compilation of activities and a celebration of diversity and inclusion.

Creative learning refers to an educational approach that emphasises creativity, innovative thinking, and a hands-on learning experience while building knowledge and developing skills. It challenges traditional teaching methodologies by integrating arts, games, and movement, encouraging students to explore and express their ideas in unique and personal ways. This approach fosters an environment where curiosity, experimentation, and risk-taking are valued, aiming to develop not only academic skills but also critical thinking, problem-solving abilities, and emotional intelligence.

The book is founded on the belief that every child has the potential to succeed and that the education system plays a crucial role in nurturing creativity. It argues that the traditional focus on rote learning and standardised testing stifles creativity and innovation. By reimagining education to prioritise creative learning, we can prepare students for a rapidly changing world. The book advocates for a curriculum that is dynamic, interdisciplinary, and inclusive, enabling every student to discover and develop their talents.

The emphasis on diversity in illustrations throughout the book is not merely an aesthetic choice but a deliberate effort to reflect the varied experiences and backgrounds of all learners. By featuring diverse characters and settings, the illustrations serve as a powerful tool for promoting inclusivity and empathy among readers. They help children see themselves and others in the activities, fostering a sense of belonging and acceptance. Moreover, diverse illustrations challenge stereotypes and broaden children's understanding of the world, contributing to their overall social and emotional development.

Each chapter of the book is meticulously designed to address different aspects of creative learning, ensuring a comprehensive exploration of the topic. From theoretical underpinnings to practical applications, the chapters build on each other to offer a holistic view of how creativity can be seamlessly integrated into education.

DOI: 10.4324/9781003515234-1

A significant focus of the book is the inclusion of Special Educational Needs and Disabilities (SEND) pupils in creative learning. Recognising that these students often face barriers in traditional learning environments, using tailored, creative approaches, teachers can cater to a wide range of learning needs. Through personalised learning experiences, the use of assistive technologies, and a supportive classroom atmosphere, creative learning can significantly enhance the educational outcomes and well-being of SEND pupils. This emphasis on inclusivity underscores the broader theme of the book: That every child deserves the opportunity to realise their potential.

Each activity has been thoughtfully crafted to ensure that every child, regardless of their abilities, can actively participate and flourish. The inclusive nature of these activities not only encourages the development of essential skills but also promotes a sense of belonging and self-confidence among young learners. In these pages, you will discover a treasure trove of innovative, imaginative, and engaging activities that transcend barriers, inviting children of all abilities to embark on a journey of discovery, growth, and wonder.

Chapter 1

DIVERSITY

Diversity is more than simply "inviting people to be in the room"; it is about ensuring that all are genuinely included and feel safe to be their whole authentic selves. But we must start by addressing the elephant in the room. Within society, inequalities, injustices, and systemic barriers marginalise groups of people. Whether it is skin colour, disability, neurodivergence, identity, class, gender, sexuality, or a mix of characteristics, these represent barriers to accessing all that society has to offer and shape the lives of people in very different ways. Having diverse voices "around the table", sharing lived experiences, and celebrating different ways of living enables us to learn more about ourselves and others.

It is our role as educators to ensure that pupils and young people learn about humanity's diversity and each person's value. Whether we share many features with a person or none at all, everyone deserves to be given the space and time to be heard. Sometimes, this raises uncomfortable questions, but to move forward, we must identify inequality, generate solutions, and actively create inclusive environments. Diversity in society represents a potential source of cultural and economic wealth if we invest time tapping into it.

Sadly, within education, we see inequality.

- A Department for Education (England) [1] literature review showed disproportionate exclusions of Black Caribbean pupils in comparison to White pupils, with pupils and parents commenting on the negative stereotypes imposed on them by White middle-class teachers.
- Pupils with special educational needs (SEN) represent 14% of the state-funded school population [2] but make up close to half of permanent exclusions [3].
- There is a disproportionate diagnosis of SEN, with a growing body of evidence showing that some ethnic and racial minority youth are more likely to receive a diagnosis of disruptive behaviour disorder and are less likely to receive a diagnosis of ADHD than their White peers [4]. This disparity leads to implications in the support provided within education and at home for these pupils.

DOI: 10.4324/9781003515234-2

- Family background, including parental education and household income, strongly predicts attainment [5]. This is shown by the percentage of young people earning a degree by age 26: 71% of private school students, compared to just 17% of the poorest fifth of families.

It is crucial for us, as teachers, to be aware of factors that impact a pupil within traditional education so that we can take steps to create an inclusive environment for all pupils.

Each activity within the diversity chapter allows pupils to learn about other people's experiences and consider how they are represented in society. By learning about this, pupils can go out into the world with a better understanding of others, reframe their attitudes, and act as allies or advocates for those around them. Over time, this forms part of a more significant effort to remove unconscious bias from society and facilitates change. One of the underlying features of this book is the illustrations, which feature pupils of different races, skin colours, religions, disabilities, genders, and more. There are adaptions and extensions to activities to ensure that all pupils can meaningfully participate in the activities.

We learn about our differences to be inclusive of everyone's experiences. A great way to explain this is using shoes! Equality means everyone gets a pair of shoes. Diversity means everyone gets a different pair of shoes. Equity means everyone gets a pair of shoes that fit. Acceptance means understanding we all wear different kinds of shoes. Belonging means wearing the shoes you want without fear of judgement.

A famous quote from Albert Einstein states, "Everybody is a genius. But if you judge a fish by its ability to climb a tree, it will live its whole life believing that it is stupid". We can apply this to all situations, questioning why we expect everyone to act the same way and achieve the same things when each person is different. Should a person using a wheelchair be expected to climb stairs? Should a person with ADHD be expected to sit still all day?

While acknowledging our differences is essential to understanding other people's experiences, we should also take the time to show how similar we all are. In the final activity, "Don't put me in a box", this is demonstrated by encouraging pupils to observe how they can be labelled in multiple ways and how each label connects them to their peers in different ways.

Note

Only some pupils can access the depth of these activities or participate in discussions around the key topics. We can support pupils' understanding and learning through storytelling. Every activity has a list of suggested books exploring the same topic. This includes books for various age groups to ensure all pupils can connect with the topic. If your class cannot fully access the activity, start by reading one of the books. You may then be able to link it to the activity.

All the activities can be used as a starting point for discussion on diversity and inclusion. Pupils might consider how the activities impact their opinions or attitudes or what they might do to take personal responsibility for creating a more inclusive society in the future.

Activities included in this chapter

Activity	Whole class	Groups	Pairs	Individuals	Extensions	Adaptions
Discover the library						
Globe spinner						
Tic-tac-toe Braille						
Guard the keys						
BSL bingo						
Lego house						
Girls or boys?						
Proud to be me						
World religions						
Don't put me in a box						

Discover the library

Inclusion is not just about ensuring everyone fits in; it's also about recognising and appreciating our differences. This activity encourages pupils to look through books in their library, identify characters who might be seen as different, and consider how they find their way in the world.

Aims

To find a book representing someone different from yourself.

Items needed per group

- Library.
- Camera, printer, glue (where photos of book covers are required).
- Coloured pens/pencils.
- Paper.

Lesson plan 1 – Whole class/small groups

- Each pupil will need a piece of paper.
- Assign each pupil a specific characteristic to look for in a book. This might be someone with a disability, someone with a different religion from me, someone with a different skin colour from me, someone who is part of the LGBTQ+ community, someone who speaks a different language from me, etc.
- Ask the pupils to find a book in the library containing the characteristics they have been given. If multiple pupils have the same one, encourage them to find different books.
- When they have their book, they should draw a large square in the centre of their paper and draw in or stick on a picture of the book's front cover.
- Around the edge, pupils will write the book's name and author, with support if required.
- They can then add other information about the book in written or picture form, such as the main character, the characteristic they identified, or what happens in the book.

- When complete, the pupils can take turns talking to a peer about the book they found, using their poster as a guide. Encourage them to try and learn something new from their peer about the book and the character.

Lesson plan 2 – Pairs/individuals

- Each pupil will make a simple booklet by folding multiple pieces of paper together.
- On each page, draw a large square about half the height and the whole width, leaving space above or below to add more information.
- Assign each page a specific characteristic which the pupil will look for in books in the library. This might be phrased as someone with a disability, someone with a different religion from me, someone with a different skin colour from me, someone who is part of the LGBTQ+ community, someone who speaks a different language from me, etc.
- Ask the pupils to find a book that matches each of the given characteristics.
- For each page, the pupils draw or stick on a picture of the cover and write the book's title.

Extension

Option 1 – Some school libraries may not have a large range of books. Using the internet or thinking of books they have at home, can the pupils suggest books that could be added to the library? This could be a list of titles, photos of front covers, or extended to a letter to the librarian.

Adaption

Option 1 – Provide pupils with a ready-curated selection of books that each feature a person representing a different characteristic.

Option 2 – Using a laptop or tablet, create a Word or PowerPoint document. Pupils may include photos, drawings, or written words.

Globe spinner

Learning about other countries, their people, and their cultures is an integral part of understanding our world. This activity takes pupils on a virtual trip to another country to learn about another culture and what it might be like to live there.

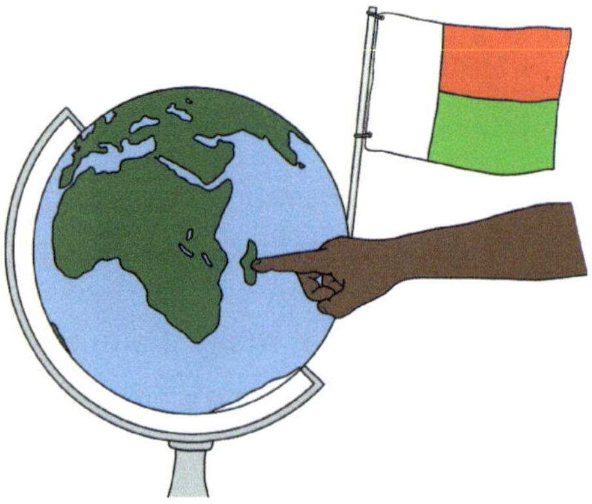

Aims

To research another country and learn about its people and culture.

Books to support learning: If the World Were 100 People by Jackie McCann, *Teatime Around the World* by Denyse Waissbluth, *Martha Maps it Out* by Leigh Hodgkinson, *A Ticket Around the World* by Melissa Owens and Natalia Diaz, *Around the World Find it! Explore it!* by National Geographic Kids.

Items needed per group

- Access to the internet.
- Globe (or globe spinner app/website).
- Paper and pens.

Lesson plan 1 – Individuals

- Each pupil will need a piece of paper.
- The pupil will create a fact file for a country. Ask pupils to draw boxes on their paper for each aspect they will examine. Ensure space for the country's name, flag, continent, and capital city. Then, add additional boxes for other information, as required. This could include fun fact(s), major religion, traditional food, language spoken, national dress, etc.
- Spin the globe with your finger pointing at it, stop it, and look at the country closest to where your finger is pointing. That is the country the fact file will be about.
- Ask the pupils to write down the country name at the top of the fact file and then fill the boxes with information using books or the internet.

Lesson plan 2 – Small groups/pairs

- Each group or pair will choose a country using the globe spinner.
- Their task is to research either the native language or a traditional dance of the country and learn a few words or dance moves. There are lots of instructional videos on YouTube to support this.
- Once they learn a little, they share the information and teach it to their peers.

Extensions

Choose one area to research further using the information found as part of the fact file. For example:

- Traditional food – create a recipe card and ingredients list.
- Language – learn a few spoken words and write them down with their translations.
- Faith and religion – find out about beliefs, prayer, rituals and clothes.

Adaptions

Option 1 (lesson plan 1) – Instead of asking each pupil to complete the research independently, do the research as a class and get them to fill out and design their fact file. You can also provide them with pre-drawn boxes or a Word document that can be edited with photos and text.

Option 2 (lesson plan 1) – Choose a few countries ahead of time, and find out the simple information about them including their flag, location on the globe, and capital city. Cut each fact or image out and mix them up. Ask your pupils to work as a team to research and sort the information to match the correct country.

Tic-tac-toe Braille

Braille is a written form of communication that uses a series of raised dots instead of letters, words, and numbers. It was created so that people who are blind or visually impaired can read by feeling the dots. A Braille cell is made up of six dots in different combinations.

Aims

To understand the purpose of Braille. To visually identify some letters of the Braille alphabet and Braille words.

Books to support learning: Six Dots by Jennifer Bryant, *The Secret Code* by Dana Meachen Rau, *Brilliant Braille* by Adam and Charlotte Guillan

Items needed per group

- Pen and paper.
- Access to the internet.

Lesson plan – Pairs

- Play a conventional game of tic-tac-toe/noughts and crosses with the pupils.
- When the grid is filled, cover one of the end columns.
- With the remainder of the grid, you have a Braille cell.
- Starting by highlighting the Os, use the internet to find out what letter, word, or number is represented by that formation of dots.
- This can be repeated multiple times by rotating the tic-tac-toe board and using Xs and Os as the focus.
- Play more games of tic-tac-toe to create more options.
- Try turning the paper over and pressing a pencil into the page where the Os are on the other side. Turn the paper back over so pupils can feel what the letter or word feels like in Braille.

Extensions

Option 1 – Ask the pupil to write their name in large letters or write it for them. Search for the Braille cell formation for each letter and draw the dots below each letter.

Option 2 – Write a simple sentence on a piece of card, leaving lots of space underneath each line of text. Underneath the words, draw out the Braille. Turn the paper over and press the pencil into the written Braille dots. Turn the paper over again and ask the pupils to run their fingers over the "Braille" created.

Adaptions

Option 1 – Create a Braille cell using a cupcake baking tray with six holes. Use tennis balls to represent the Braille dots, placing them in the wells in the tray in different positions to represent the letters. Ask pupils to feel the "dots" in the "Braille cell". This can also be done using ping-pong balls with Blu Tack to stick them to the table.

Guard the keys

Visual impairment can be considered a spectrum of sight loss conditions with differing symptoms and presentations. Some people are described as severely sight impaired (blind), others sight impaired (partially sighted), with sight loss apparent from birth or developing over time. Individuals who have lost some or all of their vision learn to rely on their other senses. This activity allows pupils to engage their other senses as they participate in a game of "dragon guarding the keys".

Aims

To engage another sense when vision is impaired. To use hearing to locate a sound.

Books to support learning: Looking Out for Sarah by Glenna Lang, *My Three Best Friends and Me, Zulay* by Cari Best, *Rainbow Joe and Me* by Maria Diaz Strom, *Keep Your Ear on the Ball* by Genevieve Petrillo

Items needed per group

- Keys on keychain.
- Blindfold.

Lesson plan – Whole class/small groups

- Talk to your class about what happens when someone loses their sight and comes to rely on their sense of hearing. Daniel Kish is an example of this. He is completely blind and uses a form of echolocation to navigate the world around him. Videos can be found on YouTube.
- Begin by asking all the pupils to sit still and close their eyes. Move around the classroom as you usually would and stop somewhere.
- Ask the pupils to listen to your movements and, without opening their eyes, point to where they think you are in the room.
- They can then open their eyes to see if they are correct.

- This sets the game scene and helps pupils understand that they need to listen for any tell-tale sounds.
- Sit everyone in a circle and place the keys in the middle.
- Choose one pupil to be the dragon who guards the keys. This pupil then sits in the middle of the circle with the keys in front of them. The pupil wears a blindfold.
- Then, a second pupil is chosen to creep around the circle, come into the centre, and steal the keys. The dragon in the centre should listen carefully and notice where the sound of the keys is.
- Once the keys have been stolen, the pupil should take their place in the circle and put the keys behind their back. All the other pupils in the circle should also put their hands behind their backs.
- The dragon removes the blindfold and tries to identify who stole the keys.

Extensions

Option 1 – Using the internet, research some causes of blindness and what someone's vision may be like with that condition. Draw a frame on a piece of card. In the space in the middle, draw the vision of someone with one of the conditions that experience it. For example, retina pigmentosa can cause tunnel vision, so cut a small hole in the centre of the frame for each eye and colour the rest of the page in black or speckled. Ask them to try holding the frame before their eyes and navigating the classroom.

Adaptions

Option 1 – Replace the keys with a shaker and have the pupil who is stealing the keys consistently shake it while they are stealing to help the dragon locate them.

BSL bingo

British Sign Language (BSL) is the sign language used in the UK by members of the deaf community. Sign language uses a mix of gestures, facial expressions, and body language. It has its own grammatical structure and syntax, which differs from spoken English. BSL is often the first and preferred language of many people within the deaf community.

Aims

To recognise the letters of the BSL alphabet.

Books to support learning: Lizzie & Lucky by Megan Rix, *Can Bears Ski?* by Raymond Antrobus and Polly Dunbar, *Moses Sees a Play* by Isaac Millman, *Max and the Millions* by Ross Montgomery, *Song for a Whale* by Lynne Kelly

Items needed per group

- BSL alphabet chart.
- BSL alphabet bingo cards (these can be made by adding photos of the signs and the letters into a table).
- Pens/pencils.

Lesson plan – Whole class/small groups

- Start by watching a video of someone demonstrating the BSL alphabet. Lots of these are available on YouTube.
- Watch a second time, pausing at each letter and letting everyone try forming it with their hands.
- Give each pupil a BSL bingo card. Let them review the signs, try forming them, and consider what they will look like when someone else signs them.
- The teacher starts by randomly choosing and signing a letter for the class. Leave time for the students to look at their cards and determine what sign you are making. You could ask pupils what letter is being shown to help those struggling.

- Continue to sign the letters randomly until a pupil crosses off a row or column and shouts bingo!
- You could also learn the sign for bingo!

Extensions

Option 1 – Using the internet, pupils could create their own version of BSL bingo, having the signs for different animals. colours, or foods rather than letters. They will need to create a comprehensive list of the words they are including, as well as create the bingo cards. This could be done by creating a table in a Word or PowerPoint document and then adding pictures of each sign.

Option 2 – Using the alphabet video and images of the alphabet, ask pupils to learn to spell their names using BSL. You could learn "My name is..." together and then add on the spelling of the name.

Adaptions

Option 1 – Make the sign with your hands and show a photo of the sign, the same as those shown on the bingo cards.

Option 2 – Reduce the number of signs on the card from the usual bingo card size to only four or six images. With four images, bingo can only be won when all four signs have been called. With six images, you could get bingo for three in a row or the whole grid.

Lego classroom

Creating spaces that are wheelchair accessible should not be difficult, although accessibility is often overlooked. Look around the room you are in, and notice any places that a person using a wheelchair could not access with ease or at all. Barriers to access include steps, narrow doorways, poor furniture placement, and inappropriate-height furniture. This activity encourages pupils to think about the changes we can make to ensure a room is accessible for everyone.

Aims

To consider the needs of a wheelchair user.

Books to support learning: Roll with It by Jamie Summer, *Winnie's Wonderful Wheelchair* by David R Morgan, *Dancing with Daddy* by Anitra Rowe Schulte, *Katy* by Jacqueline Wilson

Items needed per group

- Lego or other blocks to build with.
- Toy wheelchair or two small sets of Lego wheels to build a wheelchair (Lesson 1).
- Step (Lesson 2).
- Wooden planks (Lesson 2).

Lesson plan 1 – Small groups/pairs/individuals

- Each group will need a Lego baseplate and some Lego bricks to work with.
- The task is to create a Lego classroom with a doorway, tables and chairs, a book corner, a cloakroom, and a teacher area.
- Pupils will need to make sure the wheelchair can move freely through the classroom and access all areas,
- They may need to adjust their original design if they realise it's not suitable for a wheelchair user to access each area.

Lesson plan 2 – Small groups/pairs/individuals

- Talk to your class about how some people move around using a wheelchair. This may be one that they move themselves by pushing the wheels along (known as self-propelling) or one that is powered by an electric battery in the base.
- A German lady called Rita Ebel became known as "Lego Oma" (Lego Grandma) after making ramps for shops out of Lego bricks. She creates colourful themes so that wheelchair users, herself included, can access shops independently.
- Find a step in the classroom or create a mini-step for each group.
- Challenge the group to create a ramp using Lego. They could build a full ramp with Lego or develop a base of bricks and add planks on top.
- Remind them to think about how steep the ramp is, whether a wheelchair user could get up it and if they could roll down in a controlled way.

Extensions

Option 1 (lesson plan 1) – Give pupils a set size, such as a baseboard, within which the rooms must be contained. Give a list of items that need to be included in the build, whether there are a certain number of rooms or items within the rooms.

Adaptions

Option 1 (lesson plan 2) – Challenge pupils to walk around the classroom/school and identify places that might be difficult for a wheelchair user and what they could do to change it. This could include identifying any steps, changes in gradients of flooring, and whether or not wheelchair-accessible bathrooms are available.

Girls or boys?

It is important to learn about gender stereotyping, which is making assumptions about someone based on their perceived gender. We see gender stereotypes all around us in games, books, and on TV. This activity encourages pupils to think about what stereotypes they hold based on gender and how they might think differently.

Aims

To talk about your opinions and raise awareness of gender stereotyping.

Books to support learning: Pink is for Boys by Eda Kaban and Robb Pearlman, *Mary Wears What She Wants* by Keith Negley, *This Girl Can Do Anything* by Stephanie Stansbie, *Alien Nation* by Matty Donaldson, *There's a Boy in the Girls' Bathroom* by Louis Sachar, *The Worst Princess* by Anna Kemp

Items needed per group

- Open space.

Lesson plan – Whole class

- In the open space, ask all pupils to stand in the middle.
- Label one side of the room as "boys" and the other "girls" (for option 1 below).
- Label one side of the room as "agree" and the other "disagree" (for option 2 below).

Option 1 – Read statements from the following list and add some of your own. Ask pupils to move to the side of the room that matches their thinking. "Is this for boys, or is this for girls?"

- Burping, rescuing someone at sea, dancing, being a science teacher, cooking, liking pink, being a doctor, working with cars, liking blue, being a lawyer, cleaning the house, flying a plane, liking glitter, doing maths, having a six-pack, having long hair, being a nurse.
- Once the class has responded to each item, ask them why they made their choices. Is it true that these things are just for girls or boys, and where do these ideas come from?

Option 2 – Read statements from the following list and add some of your own. Some statements imply that girls or boys are better or more accomplished at a task or role, some imply that girls and boys are equally accomplished, and some do not relate to gender.

- Nursing is a job best suited to women. People should do a job that interests them. Boys are better at computers than girls. Boys and girls can play football at school.
- After each statement, facilitate a discussion with the pupils about whether they agree or disagree and why. They may also want to try to convince their peers to change their minds.

Extensions

Option 1 – Give pupils a statement from the list above to work from. Ask the pupils to write a paragraph explaining their thoughts in agreement or disagreement with the statement.

Adaptions

Option 1 – Add images to illustrate each of the statements you can show pupils when you present them. Label the room with illustrations to show the possibilities the pupils have.

Proud to be me

Pride is a celebration of LGBTQ+ people and their fight for equality. Pride is now being celebrated globally in over 60 countries worldwide. The community consists of a wide variety of people from all walks of life; queer people are of all races, skin colours, ages, and genders.

Aims

To understand what Pride is and who it celebrates (1). To understand that families can be made up of lots of different people (2).

Books to support learning: Mixed by Arree Chung, *And Tango Makes Three* by Justin Richardson and Peter Parnell, *Twas the Night Before Pride* by Joanna McClintick, *The Secret Ingredient* by Paul Castle, *Proud of Me* by Sarah Hagger-Holt, *The Black Flamingo* by Dean Atta

Items needed per group

- Paper – A3 paper for groups allows them all to work at the same time (1).
- Access to the internet (1).
- Coloured pens/pencils.
- Sticky notes (2).

Lesson plan 1 – Small groups/pairs/individuals

- Talk to your class about what LGBTQ+ means and the people that are included. Queer people haven't always been accepted, so Pride is a reminder to celebrate how far the community has come and work together to create a more equal society. During Pride month and Pride events, the focus is on celebrating the community and providing a place to talk about treating LGBTQ+ people with fairness and respect. These events also feature lots of music, dancing, parades, and colour.
- Show your class some images of people celebrating Pride; you could look specifically for images from an event local to you. Discuss the different outfits and people in the pictures. Note how everyone looks different but is supporting the same cause.

Option 1 – Design a costume that could be worn at a Pride event. Make sure to add lots of colours! Consider what the costume might represent, whether it's a theme after a specific flag or features all the colours of the rainbow. Encourage pupils to add interesting elements like feathers, capes, frills, and crazy hairstyles.

Option 2 – Create a poster highlighting the importance of treating everyone with kindness regardless of whether they are in the LGBTQ+ community or not. Pupils could include facts about Pride, affirmation statements, images of different people, the different Pride flags and more.

Lesson plan 2 – Whole class/ small groups/pairs/individuals

- Talk to your class about different families; the pupils can think of specific examples within their classroom. Ask pupils to take a sticky note and write/draw their family dynamic, e.g., mum, dad, brother, or a single parent.
- Pupils should then think of other families, maybe those seen in the books or on TV, e.g., mum, mamma, and write/draw them on a sticky note. Place all of the sticky notes on a large piece of paper and highlight that all of these options are families. And families don't all look the same.
- Ask the pupils what all of the families have in common and write these things on the paper around the sticky notes. This could include love, support, and an adult.

Extensions

Option 1 (lesson plan 1) – Ask the pupils to think of a way to present their poster. Working in their group/pair or alone, they should design a short presentation to talk about their poster, encourage them to be creative.

Adaptions

Option 1 (lesson plan 1) – Provide the pupils with a pre-prepared base for their poster. For option 1, this could be an outline of a person. You could also provide images of clothing that can be stuck onto their poster. For option 2, split the page into multiple boxes and provide relevant titles for each section.

World religions

Religion is part of humanity's story and continues to guide billions of people worldwide in their lives. This activity gives pupils time to explore the traditions of the major world religions and reflect on how these relate to their own way of life.

Aims

To learn about at least one major religion. To explore the fundamental beliefs and practices of at least one major religion.

Books to support learning: Hats of Faith by Medeia Cohan, *Welcome to Our World* by Moira Butterfield, and *The Usborne Book of World Religions* by Susan Meredith.

Items needed per group

- A3 paper (1).
- Access to the internet/library (1).
- Coloured pens (1).
- Interactive whiteboard/class whiteboard (2).
- Facts about each religion (2).

Lesson plan 1 – Small groups/pairs/individuals

- Split the class into seven groups, each one representing a major religion (Christianity, Islam, Buddhism, Hinduism, Sikhism, and Judaism) and one representing atheism. If pupils work in pairs or individually, more than one group will look at the same religion/group.
- Each group will need a large piece of paper, coloured pens or pencils, and access to the internet.
- Pupils should start by writing the name of the religion they are focussing on in the middle of their paper. This can be supported by providing the word to copy or trace.
- Pupils should then add information to the poster on the assigned religion. This could include drawing or printing pictures of deities, writing core beliefs, practices, and history, and drawing symbols that are used.

Lesson plan 2 – Whole class

- On the board, draw a box or column for each religion. Ask pupils to think of any religions they know and add them to the boxes. The most prominent religions are Christianity, Islam, Buddhism, Hinduism, Sikhism, and Judaism. Also, add a box for atheism.
- Go through each of the religions and ask pupils to provide information that they know about them; this could be the deities they believe in, a symbol that is used, a core belief, or a story.
- Tell the pupils the facts that you have collected and ask them to decide which religion/group each fact applies to.
- Include statements about core beliefs that are similar or different. Encourage pupils to talk about what the religions/groups might have in common or their differences.

Extensions

Option 1 (lesson plan 1) – Once the pupils have completed their poster, they should work as a group to create a presentation about the religion to give to their peers. This presentation will teach their peers about the religion they have been researching.

Adaptions

Option 1 (lesson plan 1) – Provide information about each of the religions with supporting visuals on a piece of paper. Pupils can cut out the information and stick it onto their poster, then add decorations, including images that are used within the religion.

Don't put me in a box

We often put ourselves and others into boxes, judging others broadly and unfairly based on a few factors. Maybe we look at someone and decide what they can or can't do or whether they will or won't be kind to us. This activity allows pupils to see their similarities regardless of their differences. This activity is based on a Danish TV advert called All That We Share; while it may not be appropriate for younger viewers, it holds an important message for all of us.

Aims

To acknowledge the similarities between yourself and your peers. To identify features of yourself and your peers that cannot be seen.

Books to support learning: The Same but Different by Molly Potter, *Moose Tracks!* by Karma Wilson, *Milo Imagines the World* by Matt de la Peña, *A Kids Book about Unconscious Bias* by Wendy Batchelder

Items needed per group

- Tape or chalk to mark out boxes on the ground.
- Hall or playground.

Lesson plan – Whole class

- Mark out five or six boxes on the floor around the edge of the space; they should be big enough for a group of pupils to stand in.
- Mark a "stage" area for the pupils to move to when a statement applies to them.
- Split the pupils into groups based on appearance. This could be height, hair colour, or whether they are wearing a jumper. Ask each group to stand in one of the boxes.
- Talk to the pupils about how you have separated them and how someone might make assumptions about what they can do based on how they look. Examples might include

"all the tall pupils are good at netball and basketball", "all the girls with long hair want to be princesses", and "all the boys with brown eyes are loud".

- Make a statement asking the pupils to step forward when they hear something that applies to them. When the statement is finished, they should return the box they started in.

Examples of statements could include: Step forward if ... you have a brother or sister, you like to play football, you love to read books, you have been to the zoo, your favourite colour is blue, you don't like mushrooms, you can make a piece of toast, you have held the door for someone today, you love to dance, you speak two languages.

- Finish with a statement that includes everyone, such as "Step forward if you are part of the class (name of the class)" or "Step forward if you go to (name of school)".
- It is essential to follow up on this activity with a conversation about the assumptions we make when we look at people and how inaccurate they can be; for each statement, people stepped forward from all the boxes they were allocated to at the beginning.

Adaptions

Option 1 – Instead of starting with the pupils divided into boxes, ask them to stand in a line and step forward when a statement applies, or sit down and then stand up when a statement applies to them.

Reference List

1. Graham, B., White, C., Edwards, A., Potter, S. and Street, C., 2019. School exclusion: A literature review on the continued disproportionate exclusion of certain. *Department for Education*. https://assets.publishing.service.gov.uk/government/uploads/system/uploads/attachment_data/file/800028/Timpson_review_of_school_exclusion_literature_review.pdf

2. DfE, 2018a. *Permanent and fixed period exclusions in England: 2016 to 2017, SFR 35/2017*. London: Department for Education. https://assets.publishing.service.gov.uk/government/uploads/system/uploads/attachment_da ta/file/726741/text_exc1617.pdf

3. DfE, 2018b. *Schools, pupils and their characteristics: January 2018*. London: Department for Education. https://www.gov.uk/government/statistics/schools-pupils-and-their-characteristics-january2018

4. Fadus, M.C., Ginsburg, K.R., Sobowale, K., Halliday-Boykins, C.A., Bryant, B.E., Gray, K.M. and Squeglia, L.M., 2020. Unconscious bias and the diagnosis of disruptive behaviour disorders and ADHD in African American and Hispanic youth. *Academic Psychiatry*, *44*, pp.95–102.

5. Farquharson, C., McNally, S. and Tahir, I., 2022. Education inequalities. *IFS Deaton Review of Inequalities*. https://ifs.org.uk/inequality/education-inequalities/

Chapter 2
COMMUNICATION

There are many ways in which we communicate our thoughts, ideas, opinions, and wishes to others. These, of course, include speaking and writing, but in the widest sense, this also includes music, drama, and art, each of which is distinct and separate from the others and abides by specific rules [1]. When writing, we must acknowledge the conventions of grammar and spelling to relay our message accurately. In the phonics chapter, we explore how spoken words are translated into written words by representing the speech sounds or phonemes in the word by abstract symbols, which we call letters.

In everyday life, we use communication to create connections with others. The drive to connect develops in a child's infancy firstly by eye contact and imitating the behaviour of those around them, before progressing to babbling and intentional gestures [2]. There are yet more subtle ways we communicate with others, such as body language, gestures, and facial expressions when talking.

By their first birthday, most children will produce their first recognisable word, beginning the linguistic development period. For some children, this comes naturally by reflecting what they see and hear and copying others' actions. Other children may need support to understand how to communicate with others and learn methods of communication that work for them. This can come in the form of sign language or alternative communication, such as symbol-based communication systems.

Communication is not simply expressive; there is a receptive component that makes it a two-way street. Listening is an important part of interacting with others. Children are often put in situations where they are told to listen without any preparation for learning how to listen. Active listening is more than just hearing the words and sounds but involves being actively present and engaged. Listening in this way can enhance pupils' communication skills and help them build healthy relationships. In the long term, good communication skills can improve achievement in school and adult life [3].

When communicating with others, we learn to take turns, allowing time for others to engage in the conversation. This can be difficult for young children, as they are just developing their

DOI: 10.4324/9781003515234-3

understanding of other people's points of view, which begins at around four years of age with the development of empathy [4]. Emotional recognition continues developing into late adolescence, improving social cognition [5]. This chapter allows pupils to practice turn-taking in various scenarios, including games such as "Guess the sound" and conversation-style activities such as "Conversation starter". Initiating activities that involve turn-taking also allows pupils to engage in conversations that help them learn and understand more about their peers. In addition, this chapter encourages pupils to build their confidence through tasks that involve speaking to some of their peers or to the whole class in activities like "Show and sell".

Another key aspect of communication is following and giving clear instructions, which features heavily within education. Children are often asked to complete activities by following verbal, drawn, or written instructions. Being able to follow instructions is a valuable skill to have throughout adolescence and adulthood.

When focussing specifically on communication with pupils, it is important to understand how communication develops and the hierarchy to which communication is subject [6]. There are eight non-sequential stages within communication:

- Physical real-life objects/activities.
- Objects that link to the real thing.
- Photos of the object/activity.
- Coloured illustration of the object/activity.
- Black and white line drawing of the object/activity.
- Single words.
- Phrases.
- Full sentences.

Each of these stages represents a level of understanding for the child. In different ways, they are required to generalise the information they are given and take meaning from it. For example, if they are shown a picture of a person swimming, it means they are going swimming, and so they will need to bring their swimming costume and a towel.

This chapter focusses on giving pupils the opportunity to learn individual skills that are important for effective communication, such as active listening and turn-taking. It also provides opportunities to communicate in a less pressured environment with space and time to ask questions and make mistakes.

Note

These activities can be done verbally and through signed communication but are worded with alternative communication methods in mind. You will need whatever form of communication you usually use, e.g., comm board, AAC device, or E-Tran frame, for every activity. If you are using a pre-made communication method, you may need to add subject-specific visuals to support activities. While the methods of communication below are specialised for individual needs, knowledge of their use and purpose can help support children who do not currently have communication supports in place.

Alternative communication methods

Communication board – such as a core board containing key language used in basic communication or extended language with each word supported by a photo, illustration, or line drawing.

AAC device – a high-tech option for communication, often an app on a tablet that provides multiple pages of illustrated words within topic-based folders.

E-Tran frame – a sheet of hard transparent piece of plastic with symbols or words stuck on it. It is used as a communication tool for people with limited body movement and speech but retain good control of eye movement.

Eye gaze – a high-tech option for people with limited body movement and speech but with good control of eye movement allowing them to control a computer or tablet using the movement of their eyes. This can be coupled with images or words.

Switches or buttons – large recordable buttons that can be pressed to communicate simple responses to questions or stimuli.

Activities included in this chapter

Activity	**Whole class**	**Groups**	**Pairs**	**Individuals**	**Extensions**	**Adaptions**
Guess the sound						
All about me						
Find it!						
Silly sentences						
Conversation starter						
Emotional charades						
Turn taking						
Show and sell						
Chain link pictures						
Magic carpet						

Guess the sound

Charades is all about communicating with actions and no sound. This game involves sound but no actions – and definitely no words! It gives pupils a chance to focus on listening and trying to determine the meaning of sounds. In the second lesson plan, they will need to pay attention to their peers and the sounds around them to match the sounds being made.

Aims

To use experience and the information given to make predictions and educated guesses.

Lesson plan 1 – Whole class/small groups

- One pupil will start as the "sound maker" and the others guess. They can then take turns to be the "sound maker".
- The "sound maker" needs to fold or put their arms behind their back. They cannot use their body to explain their word.
- Using their mouth, they should make a chosen sound.
- The sound could be a location, an animal, or an object.
- The other pupils should try to guess what the sound represents. It is important for them to listen to their peers to hear what has already been said and dismissed.

Lesson plan 2 – Whole class/small groups

- This activity works well if all pupils can see each other, such as when sitting in a circle.
- One pupil, the "sound maker", will need to start making a simple sound that can be replicated by their peers.
- All pupils will then need to join in making that sound.
- The "sound maker" will then slowly change the sound. The more similar the second sound is to the original sound, the harder it will be.
- Everyone else needs to pay attention to the "sound maker" and replicate the sound they make as it changes.
- Each pupil should take turns to be the sound maker for a few minutes.

Extensions

Option 1 – Give a second pupil the responsibility of deciding the sound level, how loud or quiet the sounds should be. They could signal this by moving their hands higher or lower; they could also draw the levels onto a piece of paper and indicate which one should be used. In lesson plan 1, the noise metre will apply to the sound maker; in lesson plan 2 it will apply to all pupils making noise.

Option 2 (lesson plan 2) – Ask all pupils to close their eyes or move to different areas in the classroom where they can't see each other. When the "sound maker" changes sound, they will have to rely on hearing it from the people closest to them, as the sound spreads across the room. The "sound maker" should not change the sound again until they can hear everyone making the same sound.

Adaptions

Option 1 – Provide flashcards that give ideas for the sounds to make; these could include the name of the sounds and even the sound broken down into its phonetic spelling.

Option 2 (lesson plan 2) – Display some of the chosen flashcards or sounds in a space that all pupils can see. The "sound maker" should then indicate the different sounds, and their peers should make the appropriate sound. To make it harder, start reducing the amount of time needed to make each sound and switch back and forth between different sounds.

All about me

Learning about other people is always interesting, but to start with, we need to know ourselves. This activity encourages pupils to think about themselves, what they like or don't like, and their strengths or weaknesses. It then allows them to find peers who have similar interests and learn why some of their peers think differently.

Aims

To create a positive image of themselves, allowing them to be confident and self-aware.

Items needed per group

- Paper.
- Coloured pens/pencils.

Lesson plan 1 – Individuals

- Each pupil will need a piece of paper. They should write their name at the top of the page.
- Divide the rest of the page into six boxes.
- The pupil should think of six things that are important to them or important things to know about them. You could provide suggestions for them to choose from.
- Within each box, they should write or draw the chosen thing.

Examples include a picture of me, my favourite colour, a place I like to go, what I want to be when I grow up, what my superpower would be, and something I find difficult.

Lesson plan 2 – Whole class/small groups

- Start by writing five questions on the board for all pupils to see. These should be simple questions, like number of siblings, favourite colour, job they want to do, or favourite ice cream flavour.
- Each pupil should write the numbers 1 to 5 down one side of their piece of paper.
- They then need to think about their answer to each question and write or draw it next to the appropriate number.

- After everyone has answered the questions about themselves, allow them to walk around the classroom and talk to their peers.
- The aim is to find someone for each question that has the same answer as them. If possible, it should be a different person for each question.
- When they find someone with the same answer, they should write their name or ask the peer to write their name next to it.

Extensions

Option 1 (lesson plan 2) – Complete the lesson and then ask pupils to find someone that thinks differently from them and has a different answer. They may want to talk about why they think as they do.

Adaptions

Option 1 (lesson plan 1) – Provide a premade worksheet with space for them to write their name, and then a question and supporting image in each box to guide them with their answers.

Find it!

Active listening is an important skill for children to develop, and what better way than as part of a game? Each version of this activity involves listening to a description and finding a matching picture. If they don't listen carefully, their answers won't match up.

Aims

To listen to descriptive language and locate a matching image.

Items needed per group

- Bingo cards featuring images that can be easily described, pens (1).
- Picture including lots of characters (2).
- Story picture book, it's helpful if the pupils have read the book (3).

Lesson plan 1 – Whole class

- Each pupil will need a copy of a bingo card featuring an image in each square. It is best if the cards are slightly different, either in terms of the placement of images or the included images. Each pupil will also need a pen or pencil.
- Instead of saying numbers to be crossed off, this bingo game relies on descriptions. As the adult, you will need to have a list of all of the images across all the cards.
- Start by giving simple descriptions such as something green, something found outside, or something hairy.
- When the children are comfortable with what they need to do, you can make the descriptions more complex.
- They can call "bingo!" when they have crossed off a whole row or column, and then if they cross off every image.
- When checking their card, you may need to ask them to justify crossing off an item, as some descriptions can be subjective to their environment.

Lesson plan 2 – Small groups

- All pupils will need to be able to reach the image to play a competitive "Where's Wally?"-style game. They may also want to draw a table on a separate piece of paper to keep score.
- The pupils should take it in turns to ask their peers to find something based on a description. For example, find something red.
- The others must then search the image to find something matching the description given.
- They should take it in turns to give a description.
- The game could be played with a time limit to find the objects. If no one else can find the item, the pupil who gave the description gains the point if they can show their peers an image with that description.

Lesson plan 3 – Pairs

- Pupil 1 will need to hold the book and pupil 2 will give the instructions.
- Pupil 2 starts by describing something in the book, for example, "Find something big".
- Pupil 1 then looks through the book, or the selected pages and finds something big.
- Pupil 2 then adds to the description, for example, "Find something big and red".
- Pupil 1 then has to find it; it doesn't have to be the same item as before.
- Pupil 2 should keep adding descriptors until pupil 1 can no longer find something in the book that matches the complete description.
- The pupils can then swap and try again fulfilling the opposite roles.

Adaptions

Option 1 – To support understanding of the descriptions given, you can provide pupils with flash cards containing the descriptions.

Silly sentences

Creating silly stories is a great way to exercise children's imagination. Using these methods ensures that everyone gets a chance to speak and be involved; each child's input is equally valuable and works towards the final story.

Aims

To create a silly story following a simple sentence structure.

Items needed per group

- Question cards, Who? What doing? What? Where?
- Paper, pen, dice (2).

Lesson plan 1 – Whole class/small groups

- This works best if the children are sitting in a circle and can all see the adult.
- Starting with one pupil, you will show a question card, and the children build a story by answering the questions.
- Each new question should be answered by the next child in the circle.
- The pupils will need to look at the adult to find out what part of the sentence they are thinking of and listen to their peers to hear what has already been said. You may need to prompt the beginning of some sentences to support the story's progression.
- You may want to write down the story as it is said.
- The aim is to think of sentences that sound silly and don't make sense; see the example below. The numbers signify a change in speaker.

(1) The dog (2) is cooking (3) the sofa (4) on the barbeque.

Lesson plan 2 – Pairs

- Each pair will need a piece of paper and pen to start with. Split the paper into four columns, each labelled with one of the questions. You could provide question cards to be stuck on the paper.

- Down the side of each column, write the numbers 1 to 6.
- Next to each number, write a word that matches the column heading, for example in Who?, 1. Dog, 2. Cat, 3. Girl, 4. Alien, 5. Giant, 6. Monster.
- When all of the columns have been completed, each pair will need a dice.
- One pupil rolls the dice to select a word from the first column and then passes the dice to their partner for the next column.
- They then use the selected words to form a completed sentence, which could be written down, drawn out, or spoken aloud.

Extensions

Option 1 – Add additional questions such as "How?" and "What is it like?". This will encourage pupils to extend their sentences; there is also an opportunity to build from each other's descriptions. For example, one gives a description of what something looks like, and another says what it feels like.

Adaptions

Option 1 (lesson plan 2) – The first steps could be created as a worksheet with images supporting the text for each column title and the individual words listed in each column. Pupils then start the activity by rolling the dice and then creating their silly sentences.

Conversation starter

Learning about the people around you is an important skill. The first lesson gives pupils a chance to get to know each other, ask questions of their peers, and listen to the answers. The second lesson tests the children's knowledge of their peers with a guessing game.

Aims

To engage in conversation with peers and learn something new about a classmate.

Items needed per group

- Paper and pens.

Lesson Plan 1 – Small groups/pairs

- Fold a square piece of paper into a fortune teller; instructions for this can be found online.
- On the outside, add colours or animals, and then add the numbers 1–8 on the smaller triangles.
- Under the lifted flaps, write questions or statements to start communication.

Examples include: What is your favourite animal? What country would you like to visit? What's your favourite weather? Tell me a fact about you. Tell me your proudest achievement. What frustrates you?

- Take it in turns to hold the fortune teller; the child holding it asks a peer which word to spell out, they open the fortune teller the number of times that match the number of letters in the word.
- They then ask which number they choose and read out the question under the chosen number. A teacher can support to read the question.
- Pupils can take it in turns to hold the fortune teller and their peers' questions.

Lesson plan 2 – Whole class

- Each pupil will need to write or tell the teacher a fact about themselves. It could be something their peers know or something new.
- The teacher should write each one down with the pupil's name it relates to.
- Start by bringing three pupils to the front of the class and read out their facts without saying which belongs to which pupil.
- The rest of the class should then try to guess which fact matches which of their peers.
- If two or more pupils disagree, ask them to think of what they already know about their peers and whether it matches the new facts to help them guess.
- When the final guesses have been made, ask the pupils at the front to say their facts. The aim is to match the fact with the correct pupil.
- To make it harder, have more children standing at the front.

Extensions

Option 1 (lesson plan 2) – Add an additional statement that could be about one of the children. It could be an additional fact so the class has to guess who has had two things said about them, or it could be false, and the class has to decide which statement isn't true for any of them.

Adaptions

Option 1 (lesson plan 1) – Instead of creating a fortune teller, write each question on a flashcard and put the cards face down. Take it in turns to choose a card and ask a peer a question. You can mix up the cards each turn to ensure the children can't choose a specific question.

Option 2 (lesson plan 2) – Rather than letting the children choose their own facts, ask the same question of each child brought to the front of the class.

Emotional charades

Reading body language and other people's emotions can be difficult, and expressing one's emotions can also be difficult. This activity gives children an opportunity to experiment with reading and responding to emotions without the consequences of daily life.

Aims

To guess other people's emotions and respond to them.

Items needed per group

- Emotion flashcards.
- Timer (1).

Books that support exploring emotions include: *The Colour Monster* by Anna Llenas, *The Worrysaurus* by Rachel Bright (and other dino feeling books), *I'm Happy Sad Today* by Lory Britain.

Lesson plan 1 – Whole class/small groups

- Split the class into two teams. One member of Team A starts by picking an emotion flashcard at random.
- The Team A pupil then has to act out the emotion they picked, without making any sound or speaking.
- The rest of Team A has ten seconds to guess the emotion (this time can be shortened or lengthened if the class finds it too easy or difficult).
- If Team A does not guess in time, Team B has ten seconds to guess. This continues until a team correctly guesses the emotion.
- A point is assigned to the team that guesses correctly first.
- A member of Team B is then chosen to act out an emotion and the game starts a second round.
- Continue until all of the emotion cards have been used.

Lesson plan 2 – Small groups/pairs

- One member of the group or pair will need to choose a random emotion and think about a situation when they might feel that emotion.
- That person then has to act out the situation and their emotion. They should not say what the emotion is.
- The second person or the rest of the group then need to respond to the emotion. They should think about what they would do if they were there, and what emotion they might respond with.
- After 30 seconds or so of acting out the scene, the pupils should find out what emotion was being acted to start with and tell their peer what emotions they were thinking of in response.

Extensions

Option 1 – Complete either lesson plan 1 or 2 but encourage all the pupils to keep their face blank. Attempt to act out the emotion using only body language and no facial expressions. OR complete the lesson with only facial expressions and no body language.

Adaptions

Option 1 (lesson plan 1) – Put images of each emotion in a place that can be seen by the whole class. Pupils can then use these as reference points to guess their peer's emotion.

Option 2 (lesson plan 2) – Provide the pupils with example scenarios and a matching emotion to start the acting. For example, someone snatched your favourite toy and broke it: Angry.

Turn taking

A key part of collaboration is communication. This activity removes most of the communication, allowing pupils to see what happens when they can't talk about the work they are creating together. While the final art piece can look silly and create laughs, the extensions allow for some communication elements to be restored so pupils can explore how it changes the drawings.

Aims

To create a collaborative drawing without communication.

Items needed per group

- Paper.
- Coloured pens/pencils.

Lesson plan – Whole class/small groups/pairs

- Fold a piece of paper into three equal sections; the folds should be horizontal across the paper when portrait.
- Fold enough pieces of paper for each pupil. Each pupil starts with the top of the paper. If you are using felt tips, put another piece of paper between the folded layers to catch the bleed from the pen.
- Each pupil starts by drawing and colouring the head and neck of a character. It can be completely made up or a drawing of someone or something they know. Ideally, they will not be able to or should not look at their peers' work.
- When finished, each pupil turns over the paper to the middle section ensuring the base of the neck can be seen on the middle fold.
- The pupils then swap pieces of paper, without looking at the already drawn piece.
- The pupils then draw and colour the shoulders arms and torso of a character. It does not need to be the same as the character they drew for the head.
- When finished, they turn the paper over, ensuring the base of the hips can be seen on the bottom piece of paper.

- The paper is swapped again; if in a group or class, it should be swapped with someone new.
- The pupils draw and colour the legs and feet on the paper's final section.
- Once complete, open up each piece of paper and see the final character that has been created.

Extensions

Option 1 – Follow the lesson plan a second time, but limit each starting artist to three colours; when they pass the paper around, they must also pass on the colours. When completing the activity a third time, they should pass on the three colours and tell the second artist some descriptive words about the character they started drawing. On the fourth round of drawing, open the paper after folding so the division lines show but each pupil can see what was drawn before them. Take some time after to discuss how each time they had more information about the previous artist's drawing, they could see how it changed their drawings from the first attempt when all they could see was the bottom of the previous drawing.

Adaptions

Option 1 – Draw or print full images of the entire character, head to toe. Cut each image into three at the neck and hips. Turn the pictures face down, grouped by body part. Get pupils to pick one image from each body part pile. They can then create a full character by sticking the body parts to another piece of paper. They could also try to draw and copy the character using the stuck-together images as a reference.

Show and sell

Talking about your favourite activity or person might be easy because you know lots about them, but what if you had to talk about a random object for 30 seconds? These activities encourage children to think about what is important about an object and think about using persuasive and descriptive language.

Aims

To persuade a peer that they need or want a random object.

Items needed per group

- Random objects.
- Timer.
- Paper and pens (2).

Lesson plan 1 – Small groups/pairs

- One pupil starts as the seller, and the others are the customers.
- The seller chooses a random object from within the classroom. They have 30 seconds to describe the object and discuss why their peers might want it. They could talk about how bright the colour is, or how useful it might be.
- The customers then discuss or think about whether or not the seller convinced them. They might want to ask the seller a question about the object to learn more.
- The pupils can then switch around and each try out being the seller.
- At the end, they can decide what made one pupil's sale more interesting than another. They can think of what should be included to make more people want the random object.

Lesson plan 2 – Small groups/pairs/individuals

- To start with, the pupils will need to choose a random object and draw it in the middle of the piece of paper.
- They then need to think of the key features of the object and draw/write them around the rest of the paper.

- Once completed, each group/pair/individual should try to sell their object to another member of the class, using their poster as a starting point.
- Set a timer for 30 seconds to sell the object; if in a group they probably have time for one or two sentences each.
- Remind them to refer to the key points that they came up with for their poster.

Extensions

Option 1 – A lot of communication is in our tone of voice and body language. Two pupils will need to try to sell the same object to a group or the class. One pupil should be instructed to be loud and exciting. The second pupil should do the presentation standing completely still and trying to keep their voice monotone. After the presentations are done, ask the rest of the class what the difference was and which one they would want to buy from more.

Adaptions

Option 1 – Choose the objects first and provide the class with questions to guide their sales. These could include: What does it look like? What is it useful for? How do you use it? The questions could be paired with images to support comprehension.

Chain link pictures

Listening to instructions and carrying them out is important. Trying to replicate the instructions again and again questions the accuracy of the instructions given. This activity gives children an idea of what it's like to pass information on and how it can change the more people hear it and pass it on.

Aims

To give accurate instructions. To listen to and act on instructions given.

Items needed per group

- Paper.
- Pens/pencils.

Lesson plan – Small groups/pairs

- Each pupil will need a piece of paper and a pen. This activity works best when the pupils can't see each other's work, but they will need to hear the person before them.
- The first pupil will need to draw something simple on their piece of paper.
- The first pupil then describes their drawing to the second pupil, who cannot see the initial drawing.
- The pupils continue describing the drawing until each group member has a drawing described by the pupil before them.
- At the end, they should compare all of the drawings and then examine the differences between the first and last drawings.
- The game can be repeated with a different pupil starting. It could be made more difficult by setting a timer for the pupils to describe their drawings.

Lesson plan – Whole class

- The teacher or one pupil starts by drawing a simple image on a piece of paper that the rest of the class can't see.
- Each class member will need a piece of paper and a pen/pencil.
- They then give clear instructions to the rest of the class.

- The class members each listen to the instructions and draw on their piece of paper following the instructions.
- Once finished, the pupils can compare their images. They will likely see that each of their images is slightly different. Their interpretation of the instructions will be slightly different unless the instructions are completely accurate and easy to understand.

Extensions

Option 1 – To make the game harder, use a more complicated drawing, for example adding swirls or patterns. You could also add different colours that are passed to the person drawing each turn.

Adaptions

Option 1 – Give the pupils some cut-out shapes that can be arranged on a piece of paper to form the image. Instead of needing to draw their picture, they move the correct shapes onto the page in the locations described by their peer.

Magic carpet

Magic carpets are a great part of storytelling and often lead characters on amazing adventures. Use your pupils' imaginations to take them on a flight across the world by working as a team to solve problems and continue the story.

Aims

To listen to instructions and problem-solve with their peers to complete a task.

Items needed per group

- One sheet, tarp, or blanket per group.
- Large space, e.g., hall or playground.
- Items to support the story, e.g., chair, blocks.

Lesson plan – Small groups

- This activity can be completed with one teacher giving instructions and the children split into small groups of up to six pupils.
- Each group will start with their sheet laid out flat on the floor, and all team members will stand or sit on top.
- The teacher's job is to tell a story about the magic carpet and its destinations. Pupils may need to change the shape of the sheet, stand in specific ways to pass through doors, or give passwords.
- The activity works best when the teacher creates an elaborate story, encouraging pupils to use their imagination.
- When each instruction is given, the pupils must work together to solve the problem. They cannot step off the sheet.
- You can use rhyme, magic words, or sounds to support the story.

Examples include:

Turn the carpet completely upside down without stepping off.

The carpet is approaching a tunnel, you can only be two people wide and must crouch down to avoid hitting the ceiling.

You are heading towards a forest; you need to fold the carpet in half to fit through the gaps between trees.

To get through the gate, the carpet must be square.

To pass the volcano, you must press and hold the buttons on each end side of the path (put a chair a little away from the sheet on each side; pupils can work together to balance and touch both chairs).

Your carpet is approaching a thin canyon, so you need to stand in a single file facing one side of the carpet.

Extensions

Option 1 – Complete the challenges but don't let the pupils speak to each other. They must concentrate on body language and gestures and guide each other.

Adaptions

Option 1 – Use a bigger sheet to allow more space for pupils to move around.

Option 2 – Have a supporting adult on each sheet to support communication and help pupils understand the instructions.

Reference list

1. Dimbleby, R. and Burton, G., 2020. *More than words: An introduction to communication*. London: Routledge.

2. Ferreira, S. and Cruz-Santos, A., 2021. A review and analysis of four measures of early childhood communication development. *SN Social Sciences*, *1*(5), p.100.

3. Umida, M., 2024. Enhancing listening skills in primary school students. *American Journal of Interdisciplinary Research and Development*, *28*, pp.253–260.

4. Decety, J., 2010. The neurodevelopment of empathy in humans. *Developmental Neuroscience*, *32*(4), pp.257–267.

5. Tonks, J., Williams, W.H., Frampton, I., Yates, P. and Slater, A., 2007. Assessing emotion recognition in 9–15-years olds: Preliminary analysis of abilities in reading emotion from faces, voices and eyes. *Brain Injury*, *21*(6), pp.623–629.

6. Park, K., 1997. How do objects become objects of reference? A review of the literature on objects of reference and a proposed model for the use of objects in communication. *British Journal of Special Education*, *24*(3), pp.108–114.

Chapter 3 VOCABULARY

Learning vocabulary is important in developing our students' language, but it cannot be taught through books and conversations alone. By using interesting media and diverse activities, we can allow students to enjoy and be more interested in learning vocabulary. This chapter will guide you through activities that can be used within your classroom to support pupils in building their language skills.

Studies have shown that using imagery alongside vocabulary learning has a positive impact on memory retention of new words, in addition to making learning more engaging as the imagery attracts students' attention [1–3]. The activities in this chapter allow students to identify new words and understand them through imagery. The activity adaptions often include visuals or object supports; the purpose is explained through the hierarchy of communication, as mentioned in the communication chapter. The hierarchy of communication works on the assumption that physical objects and photos are the easiest to comprehend due to their similarities and links to the referenced object or activity. Words, phrases, and sentences are the most complex to understand, with illustrations linking the two areas together.

Engaging in group discussions, role-playing scenarios, and language games is an effective way to improve communication skills and reinforce learning new vocabulary [4]. These interactive activities help students expand their linguistic repertoire and foster a passion for language acquisition. The confidence and skills gained from these activities can positively impact other areas of learning, such as acquiring a second language, participating in debates, or taking on roles in student representation, like joining a school council.

In addition, learning vocabulary is important for students who are learning to read. When reading, students blend individual sounds together to form the word; having a larger vocabulary supports students with the final pronunciation and understanding of the word they are reading. Reading words accurately supports comprehension, which in turn supports engagement with the text and allows further access to the language [5]. The importance of this comprehension is highlighted in Scarborough's Reading Rope [6]. Scarborough states that a skilled reader comprises of multiple elements. The first is language comprehension,

DOI: 10.4324/9781003515234-4

which consists of background knowledge, vocabulary, language structures, verbal reasoning, and literacy knowledge. The second is word recognition, which is explained further in the chapter on phonics. The extensions for the activities include ways to make the activity harder or extend the activity to further develop the pupil's thinking on the topic. These may contribute further to the other areas in the language comprehension section of Scarborough's Reading Rope.

Semantics of language

Specific questions can focus on different elements of language and guide pupils to the relevant vocabulary. These questions can extend pupils' thinking about the language they are exposed to and provide a simple framework for their own language formation.

Who? The character of the sentence, a person, animal, or animated object.
What are they doing? The action of the character.
What? The object used as part of the action.
Where? The location of the character, action, or object.
What next? The connective language used to extend sentences.
How? Descriptions of the character, object, or location.
What is it like? Descriptions of the character, action, object, or location.
Who(se) is it? The pronouns of the character.
When? The time at which the action is happening.
Did/Going to do what? Exploring the action in alternative tenses.

Activities included in this chapter

Activity	Whole class	Groups	Pairs	Individuals	Extensions	Adaptions
Exploring books						
Vocabulary match						
Treasure hunt walkabout						
Small world						
Treasure map						
Mystery box						
Food shop						
Word search						
Would you rather?						
Where is it?						

Exploring books

Visuals are a clear aid to comprehension; we see this in children's books, both fiction and nonfiction, through photos and illustrations. This activity uses visuals to support pupils in understanding the meaning of the words they are using and gives them tools to break down sentences to improve comprehension.

Aims

To identify key language within a book. To create sentences or a story using visual supports.

Items needed per group

- Books with clear character and action sentences. Fiction stories will work best for extension activities; however, nonfiction can also be used.
- Vocabulary cards relating to the book, plus additional for extension activities (characters, actions, objects, descriptions).

Initial lesson plan

- Read the book one page at a time. At the end of each page, pause to ask relevant questions about the characters and their actions. For example: What is the cat doing? What colour is the dog? Who is eating the chocolate?
- For each page, identify the key characters, their descriptions, and their actions.
- Using the vocabulary cards, make sentences about the story using a joint space such as a whiteboard.
- Assign sounds and actions to the characters and their sentences

Example: The cat [meow] prowled [tiptoe] through the long grass [swish sound and sway arms].

Option 1 – Whole class/small groups

- Split the class into groups (or the group into individuals) and assign each a character, and one the narrator.
- The narrator(s) says the sentence supported by the visuals.

- Each group/individual acts out the sentence following the assigned actions and sounds.
- Complete for each page that sentences have been written for until the whole story can be told in this manner.

Option 2 – Pairs/individuals

- Identify the characters and work together/alone to build sentences for a single page of the book.
- The whole story could be told by using work from each pair or individual.

Extensions

Option 1 – Record the enactment of each page of the book and edit together to create the full story. Try mixing up the clips and seeing what difference it makes to the story.

Option 2 – Write out the sentences for one page of the book and add drawings to show comprehension. A page could be assigned to different pupils, and all brought together to create the full story.

Option 3 – Discuss or write about how the story could end differently if a character changed their actions. What would happen if all their positive actions became negative? What would happen if they talked instead of ran, or jumped instead of drinking?

Vocabulary match

This activity targets both short- and long-term memory by providing new information in the form of the cards' location and encouraging pupils to access old information in the form of the images on the cards. It also provides an opportunity to identify patterns in the images, in addition to supporting fine motor skills in picking up and turning over the cards.

Aims

To utilise short-term memory by identifying the correct cards once they are no longer visible. To take turns and allow others to play uninterrupted. To learn the meaning of new words.

Items needed per group

- Two sets of vocabulary cards.

Lesson plan 1 – Small groups/pairs

- Lay out one set of the vocabulary cards, picture side up. Identify the image and talk about what it is, the context it may be found in, and examples of the word in a sentence.
- Mix up the two sets of cards and lay them face down on the table. The more pairs used, the harder the game will be.
- Take it in turns to turn over two cards with the aim to collect matching cards.
- If you are correct, you keep the cards. If the cards do not match, leave them in place and turn them back over.
- When all cards have been matched, the winner is the pupil with the most cards.

Lesson plan 2 – Individuals

- Turn over two cards at a time. If they match, put the pair aside. If not, turn them back over and try again until you have matched all of the pairs.
- An extension would be to write a sentence about each word on a pair of cards you find.

Extensions

Option 1 – To keep a matched pair, the pupil must say a sentence that includes the word pictured. If they cannot, the cards must be returned to the game. Add a timer to make this more difficult.

Option 2 – To keep a matched pair, the pupil must think of a word that rhymes with the word pictured. If they cannot, the cards must be returned to the game. To play this version, ensure that all words being used have rhymes within the capability of the pupils. Add a timer to make this more difficult.

Adaptions

Option 1

- Use one set of vocabulary cards face down on the table. Next to the cards, you will need the physical object that matches the cards. An example is having flashcards of animals and then using toy animals as the objects.
- Take it in turns to turn over a card and identify the matching object. If the pupil is correct, they keep the card and object, if not they must return the card and object to the game.
- The player with the most card and object matches at the end of the game is the winner.

Option 2 (for extension 1)

- Offer sentences with gaps where the words from the cards would fit.
- When a pupil finds a matching pair within the game, they must choose the correct sentence for the words they have found.

Example: The word is pasta. Eating ______ makes me happy. I love to go to the ______.

Treasure hunt walkabout

Providing an opportunity to follow instructions teaches pupils their own responsibility and ability to complete a task. The activity also works on vocabulary development and receptive language skills.

Aims

To engage with all five senses to identify the features of an object. To communicate with peers and solve problems together (group). To work independently following instructions (individual).

Items needed per group

- Paper or whiteboards and pens or the ability to take photos.
- Objects around the classroom or playground.

Lesson plan 1 – Whole class

- Create a list of descriptions such as colours or textures to describe objects around the classroom/playground.
- Split the class into small groups; each are given a list of items to find. To reduce the amount of copying, you can give each team a slightly different list or tell pupils that they will earn an additional point if no-one else finds the same object.
- Set a timer for the pupils to collect as many items as they can together before time runs out, or set the pupils against each other to see which pupil can collect all the items first.

Lesson plan 2 – Individuals

- Each individual should have their own list. You may want to use a variety of different lists to encourage pupils to work independently or tell pupils that they will earn an additional point if no-one else finds the same object.
- Set a timer for the pupils to collect as many items as they can together before time runs out, or set the pupils against each other to see which pupil can collect all the items first.

Extensions

Option 1 – Ask the pupils to add descriptions of the objects not included in the instructions. For example, if the instructions asked them to find objects of a specific colour, can they describe the texture, size, or shape of each of the objects they found.

Option 2 – Each group or individual works to write their own treasure hunt for other members of the class. Encourage them to focus on object items or one specific descriptor for the items. They should check that their treasure hunt can be completed by finding all of the objects themselves. The new lists can be photocopied and redistributed for other class members to have a go. This also gives an opportunity for peer feedback on the treasure hunts after they are completed.

Adaptions

Option 1 – Instead of writing a list of descriptions or objects, draw or find photos of the descriptions. This works well when looking for items of a specific colour or shape.

Small world

Storytelling brings to life the language learnt, enabling development and encouraging pupils to think beyond their own viewpoint and express their viewpoint to others.

Aims

To identify the basic elements of a story and use them to create a story. To identify the beginning, middle, and end of a story, and identify the characters, settings, and events.

Items needed per group

- Variety of toys to suit location.
- Materials that can be used to represent places, e.g., sand, soil, oats, rice, newspaper, stones, foil, plants, playdough, tissue paper.

Lesson plan 1 – Small groups

- Set up an area and create a "small world" using classroom items and materials. Stick to a theme or location, such as the beach, space, forest, zoo, farm, or playground.
- Add toys that act as the characters; they should be relevant to the location.
- Ensure all the pupils involved can reach the play area.
- Let the students play with the characters creating their own stories. Encourage them to vocalise what they are doing, the characters, descriptions, actions, and intentions. Pupils can work independently to create their own storyline or work together coming up with a story as a group.
- The supporting adult should ask questions that guide the pupils to explore new ideas; they may also offer new words that are relevant to the pupils' story. They should not take charge of the storyline or assume what the pupils are doing.

Lesson plan 2 – one-to-one

- Set up an area and create a "small world" using classroom items and materials. Stick to a theme or location such as the beach, space, forest, zoo, farm, or playground.
- Add toys that act as the characters; they should be relevant to the location.

- Let the pupil lead the story telling. The adult should ask open questions encouraging the pupil to grow their story. The adult may also offer new words and comment on what the pupil is doing.

Extensions

Option 1 – Give the pupils an empty storyboard after their time playing with the small world, and ask them to draw and write the story. The storyboard could be made by the whole group, or each individual pupil writes their own.

Option 2 – Have a half-completed storyboard involving the characters and scene that you have set up. Draw and write half of the story board up until a "main event" has been identified. Encourage the pupils to play following the story board and then play out different endings. Which end do they think is most likely? What might a funny ending be? They can then take a copy of the storyboard and write out their favourite ending.

Adaptions

Option 1 – Create an aided language board for the small world that includes the important words needed to create commentary about the characters. This should include the characters, actions, objects, and descriptions; more can be added depending on the level of the pupils. While playing with the small world, the adult can point and verbalise words using the aided language board as well as encouraging pupils to use the aided language board as a prompt for their story telling.

Treasure map

This activity encourages pupils to acknowledge and study their environment while recalling directional language that will help them give and receive instructions. When working in pairs, this activity also supports active listening.

Aims

To use directional and descriptive language to guide a peer towards a specific item or location. To develop spatial awareness by mapping out an area and its obstacles.

Items needed per group

- Pens and squared paper.
- Indoor or outdoor space with obstacles.

Lesson plan 1 – Pairs

- Each pupil will need a piece of paper and some pens or pencils.
- Pupils should work together to draw the space including any obstacles, walls, and doors. Remind pupils to be aware of the size of objects and to use the squares on the paper as reference. You may want to show examples such as a table being 8 by 4 squares and a chair being 2 by 2 squares.
- One pupil in each pair should be shown the start and end points. You may want to use a variety of points to ensure there is space for each pair to complete the activity.
- They should direct their peer to navigate the room using the map and the allocated start and end. The peer being given instructions should not be told the end point.
- Encourage pupils to use directional language such as left, right, forward, backward.
- When one pupil has directed, give the other pupil a second end point and they can swap who is in charge of directions.

Lesson plan 2 – Individual

- Create a simplified map of the space on the squared paper with obstacles; these could include chairs, tables, and play equipment.

- Give the pupils a starting point and an end point.
- The pupils need to work out how to navigate the map to avoid obstacles and get to the end.
- Pupils should draw their directions onto the map following the squares. They should ensure that they navigate around obstacles and that there is space for them to do so.
- Encourage pupils to use directional language such as left, right, forward, backward.
- Ask pupils to check their own maps by following the instructions and making changes if needed.

Extensions

Option 1 – Tell pupils that they must include a certain number of instructions in their directions. Examples include using a specific number of turns, navigating a certain number of obstacles, or doing one movement that is not walking such as jumping or crawling.

Option 2 – Tell pupils to find the shortest possible route with the least amount of turns and obstacles encountered.

Adaptions

Option 1 – Provide pupils with a map that already has the route mapped out. Ask pupils to follow the map and note how they know they are in the right place. They could also write down the instructions they would use to talk someone else through the map. This could be using words or images such as arrows.

Mystery box

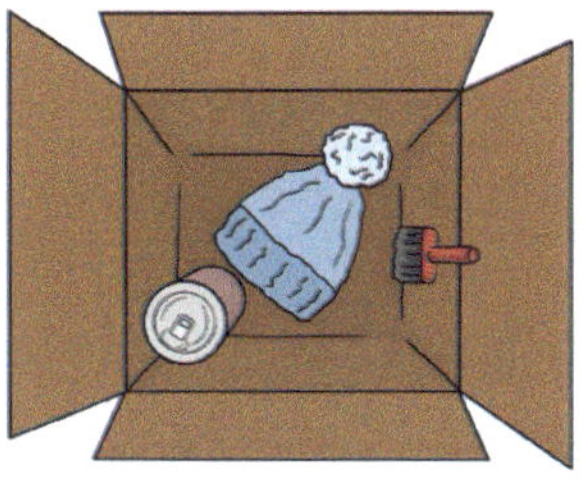

Pupils have to actively listen to the descriptions and answers of others to make an informed guess about the object. This activity encourages pupils to use all of the available information, including the descriptions given, and other pupils' guesses and answers to their questions to make an informed guess about the object.

Aims

To recall relevant descriptive language based on the sensory inputs of an object. To gain information through asking relevant questions.

Items needed per group

- Opaque bag or box.
- Random objects.

Lesson plan 1 – Whole class/small groups/pairs

- This activity works well if the students can sit in a circle/opposite each other. Place an object into the box, and give the box to the first student.
- The pupil should feel inside the box.
- The pupil should start describing how the object feels, its shape, size, and texture.
- The other pupils should try and guess what the object is based off the information given.
- If the item is not guessed, the pupil with the box may then look at the object ensuring no one else sees. They can then describe what the object looks like and what it might be used for.
- Encourage the other pupils to guess what the object might be.
- Add a time limit for the descriptions to make the game harder.
- Change the object and give the box to another pupil to play again.

Lesson plan 2 – Whole class/small groups/pairs

- This activity works well if the pupils can sit in a circle/opposite each other. Place an object into the box, and give the box to the first pupil.
- The pupil should feel and look inside the box.

- The other pupils should take it in turns to ask yes or no questions about the object. They can also make guesses of what the object might be based on the answers.
- The pupil with the box should only say the words yes or no until the object is guessed.
- Change the object and give the box to another pupil to play again.

Extensions

Option 1 – Give each pupil a blank piece of paper and pens or pencils. Ask them to choose one of the objects and draw it in the centre of the page. They should then add labels of the descriptions used to guess the object in the game; this could be writing words or adding small additional drawings of each description.

Adaptions

Option 1 – Provide the pupils with an aided language board or vocabulary cards of the descriptions they could use for the object as a prompt.

Option 2 – Put a selection of photos or drawings of objects for the pupils to choose from including the hidden object. Using the description or answers to the questions, students can choose the image they think represents the hidden object.

Food shop

This activity is a direct link to real life and can be used as part of a cooking lesson or helping a family make a meal. Identifying relevant information is a useful skill that can be used in a variety of scenarios and engages pupils in reading actively.

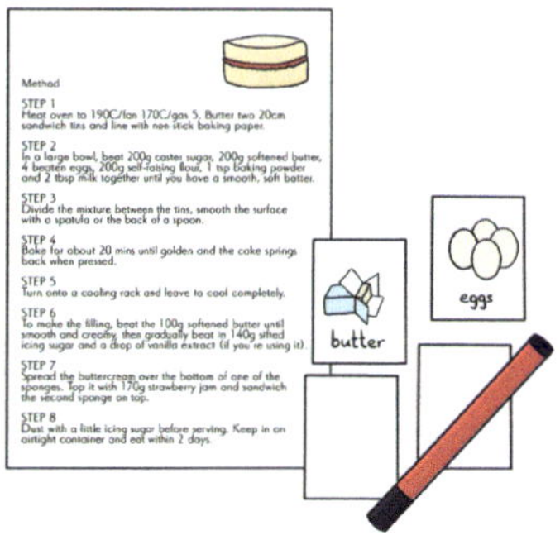

Aims

To comprehend a set of instructions by searching for specific types of words. To create a list of ingredients from a set of instructions.

Items needed per group

- Recipes that match your pupils' reading level or a recipe that is supported by visuals. You will only need the method.
- Pens and paper.

Lesson plan 1 – Small group

- Give each pupil within a group a different recipe. They only need to be slightly different e.g., peanut butter sandwich, jam sandwich, and ham sandwich.
- Each pupil should create flash cards of the ingredients they need for their recipe, each ingredient on its own card. These could be drawn or written.
- When finished, all of the flash cards should be mixed together, and pupils should swap to different recipes.
- Following their new recipe, the pupils should look for the items they need in the flashcards.
- Encourage pupils to notice if they are missing ingredient cards or if they have collected enough cards.

Lesson plan 2 – Individual

- Give each pupil a recipe.
- Ask the pupils to look through their recipe and highlight the ingredients that they would need.
- Ask pupils to write a list and illustrate the ingredients they have identified.

Extensions

Option 1 – Ask pupils to look for tools they would need to complete the recipe e.g., plate, mixing bowl, spoon. And complete the activity as above. This is likely to be harder and cause more differences, as recipes often don't state every piece of equipment needed.

Option 2 – Having read the recipe and identified the ingredients, ask the pupils to identify something that could be changed or added to make it better. An example could be adding butter to a jam sandwich, adding yoghurt to a fruit salad, or chocolate chips to pancakes. They should identify the ingredient and think of a reason why it would make the recipe better.

Adaptions

Option 1 – Provide pupils with premade flash cards of a variety of ingredients including items they don't need for their recipe. Pupils can work alone or in pairs to find the correct ingredients for their recipe.

Word search

This activity allows pupils to differentiate the different types of words and expand their vocabulary by thinking of alternatives to the words provided.

Aims

To identify action words when reading or listening to a set of instructions. To think of alternative action words that mean the same or different to the original word.

Items needed per group

- Recipe that matches your pupils' reading level or a recipe that is supported by visuals. You will only need the method.
- Pens and paper.

Lesson plan 1 – Whole class/small groups

- Choose a recipe to look at as a class. Put it up on the board so all students can see.
- Read through the recipe and play "stop the bus". As you read, ask the pupils to shout out "stop the bus" when you reach an action word.
- When you stop, highlight or underline the action words.
- At each word, ask your pupils if they can think of an alternative action word that would create the same action. For example, mix changes to stir, weigh changes to measure, and bake changes to cook.

Lesson plan 2 – Pairs

- Give each pupil a different recipe.
- Ask pupils to look through their recipe to identify and highlight the actions used e.g., mix, weigh, bake.
- Pupils will then need to re-write the recipe leaving a gap where the action words are supposed to be. You can specify how many words they replace and how many are left as normal or ask them to replace all the action words.
- Then ask pupils to fill the gaps with the wrong action words such as replacing mix with hug or bake with freeze.

- When the pupils have finished writing the new recipe, they swap with their partner.
- Looking at the new recipe, the pupils should identify the action words that don't fit with the instructions.
- The pupils then need to try and work out the correct word based on the other language around it.

Extensions

Option 1 – Give pupils an item they know how to make, such as a sandwich or fruit salad. Ask them to write a set of instructions to make the item.

Adaptions

Option 1 – Provide pupils with a list of actions that are usually used within the type of recipe you are looking at, along with a variety of other actions they could use as substitutes.

Option 2 (extension 1) – provide pupils with the individual instructions to make an item. Ask pupils to put the instructions in the correct order to complete the recipe.

Would you rather?

This activity strengthens skills in interpersonal influence, problem-solving, and verbal reasoning. Pupils are encouraged to have their own opinions, defend them, and understand others' points of view.

Aims

To develop an argument based on opinions and facts. To complete an oral presentation using persuasive language. To understand an argument from another person's point of view.

Items needed per group

- Open space (for whole class lesson).
- Images to support discussion.

Lesson plan 1 – Whole class

- Ask a simple "would you rather" question to the class. Ask those that agree with answer 1 to move to one area, and those that agree with answer 2 to move to another area.
- Ask a pupil in each group why they chose as they did.
- Ask another pupil in each group what they would say to convince someone on the other side to change their mind.
- Ask the pupils to change sides if they think the other team made a good argument and they have now changed their mind.
- Bring the pupils back to the centre and ask another question to play again.

Lesson plan 2 – Groups/pairs

- Split the pupils into two teams (two individuals).
- Ask a "would you rather" question giving two answers. Assign each team one of the answers, and explain that it doesn't matter if they agree with the answer they were given, but it is their job to convince you that it is the "right" answer.
- Give the pupils time to work together (or alone) to come up with a list of reasons why the answer they have is "right".
- Ask the pupils to also think about reasons why the other teams answer is "wrong".

- When the teams are done, set up a mini debate, and ask each team to make points about their answer or the other teams. They should take it in turns to respond and explain their reasons.
- If doing in front of a whole class, the rest of the class could vote at the end of the debate on the answer they think is "right".
- It's important to talk about how people have different opinions and people are allowed to like and believe different things.

A good example of this activity is choosing colours as the answers. Would you rather have blue skin or green skin? It's completely irrelevant to general life but engages pupils in the argument and allows them to think about the other perspective without pre-determined opinions.

Extensions

Option 1 – Pupils can work independently to write a piece of persuasive writing or record a persuasive video to convince you or one of their peers of their point of view.

Option 2 – Pupils will need a piece of paper; they will need to draw a line down the centre. Write or draw an argument on each side of the line. Ask pupils to write or draw arguments for both sides that directly combat each other. For example, blue skin would be better to hide in the ocean, green skin would be better to hide in the forest.

Adaptions

Option 1 – Set up a tournament of "Would you rather?". Start by asking eight questions, then pit the winners of each question against each other until there is only one left. This can be done easily with visual prompts.

Where is it?

Aims

To identify and define prepositions and locate them in the world around them. Differentiate between an object of the preposition and other objects.

Items needed per group

- Object e.g., ball or box (one per student).
- Flashcards can be used to remind students of the prepositions (1).
- Pens and paper (2,3).
- Images of individual objects on paper (2).

Lesson plan 1 – Whole class/small groups

- The activity is to play Simon Says as a class. Start with an adult giving instructions, then let pupils have a go at being Simon.
- Each instruction should include a preposition, the person, and an object.
- Examples include, Simon says the ball is "on" your head. Simon says you are "next to" the ball. Simon says you are "above" the ball.
- To make it more difficult, you can tell students that prepositions cannot be repeated.

Lesson plan 2 – Pairs/individuals

- This activity is a scavenger hunt following instructions or questions that direct pupils to find pictures of objects.
- Pupils should be given a list of instructions that create a scavenger hunt around the classroom or playground. To reduce copying, you could mix up the order of the instructions or give out a variety of lists.
- Examples include: What is behind the whiteboard? Look in the sink. Is there anything under the water bottles? Check on top of the teacher's desk. What is near the door?
- Include a mix of statements and questions, use a variety of prepositions, and vary the place of the preposition in the sentence.

Lesson plan 3 – Pairs

- Pupil 1 should draw a room on a piece of paper. They could do this from a person's point of view or as a room plan. Pupil 2 should not see the drawing.
- When the drawing is complete, pupil 1 should describe the room to pupil 2.
- While listening to the description, pupil 2 should draw what they hear.
- Pupil 1 will need to use locational prepositions to explain the placement of items in the room.
- When pupil 1 has finished describing, they should compare drawings and see if there are any inconsistencies.
- Pupils may need to talk about changes they need to make or how the drawing could have been better described.

Extensions

Option 1 (lesson plan 2) – Ask pupils to create their own scavenger hunt. They could draw items to hide around the classroom and write a list of instructions to find them. Pupils can work together to create their hunt or work alone. They can then swap instructions and try out each other's hunts.

Adaptions

Option 1 – For each activity, provide pupils with additional vocabulary cards to the prepositions; these can be used to create full sentences. For lesson plan 1, this would be a person and the object (e.g., ball). For lesson plan 2, this would be pieces of furniture or items in the classroom. For activity 3, this would be pieces of furniture and items that may be found in the room the student has chosen to draw.

Reference List

1. Liando, N.V.F., Tatipang, D.P., Tamboto, G., Poluan, M. and Manuas, M., 2022. Pictures as a learning media in teaching vocabulary. *Jurnal Ilmiah Universitas Batanghari Jambi, 22*(3), pp.1944–1949.

2. Birinci, F.G. and Saricoban, A., 2021. The effectiveness of visual materials in teaching vocabulary to deaf students of EFL. *Journal of Language and Linguistic Studies, 17*(1), pp.628–645.

3. Mohd Tahir, M.H., Safinas Mohd Ariff Albakri, I., Mohd Adnan, A.H., Syafiq Ya Shak, M. and Mohamad Shah, D.S., 2020. The application of visual vocabulary for ESL students' vocabulary learning. *Arab World English Journal (AWEJ), 11*, pp.323–338.

4. Alshraideh, D.S. and Alahmdi, N.S., 2020. Using drama activities in vocabulary acquisition. *International Journal of English Language Teaching, 7*(1), p.41.

5. Hashemi, A., 2021. The effects of using games on teaching vocabulary in reading comprehension: a case of gifted students. *Journal for the Education of Gifted Young Scientists, 9*(2), pp.151–160.

6. Scarborough, H.S., Neuman, S. and Dickinson, D., 2009. Connecting early language and literacy to later reading (dis) abilities: Evidence, theory, and practice. *Approaching Difficulties in Literacy Development: Assessment, Pedagogy and Programmes, 10*, pp.23–38.

Chapter 4
PHONICS

Phonics is the foundation of reading and spelling. Written language is described as a code that uses the alphabet, where letters stand for the sounds in spoken words. A systematic synthetic phonics programme is the most effective way to teach phonics [1]. When we write and spell a word, we think of the sounds in the word and represent them with a letter or group of letters. When reading, we do the reverse; we look at the letters, match the sounds, and blend them to get the word. Phonics programmes teach children how the code works, the relationship between sounds and letters, and the key blending and segmenting skills. Programmes start simply, with short words where single letters match sounds, moving on to longer and more complex words where sounds are represented by more than one letter and where sounds are represented in more than one way.

The DfE's Reading Framework [2] highlights the social, cultural, and economic importance of reading, with the national curriculum programmes of study based on a conceptual model consisting of language comprehension and word recognition. It is vital that the early and successful teaching of phonics is complemented throughout the school years by promoting reading comprehension and fluency. The Reading Framework also highlights the need to engage pupils who are struggling with reading early on, as they may be "put off" reading, which further impacts their progress.

Skilled reading is made up of multiple elements. This is illustrated by Scarborough's Reading Rope [3], which describes how we need to teach word recognition and develop reading comprehension. This chapter focusses on word recognition and includes activities that work on phonemic awareness, decoding (reading), and encoding (spelling), and how they support the development of reading automaticity. In addition, there is an activity that works on letter formation. This is achieved through fun games that engage pupils and are highly motivational. A 2023 study [4] explored the link between using games in phonics instruction and students' motivation to learn. The study found that pupils were more motivated to learn when games were used as part of the teaching and learning process.

DOI: 10.4324/9781003515234-5

Of significant importance in phonics teaching is repetition, especially when a pupil has special educational needs. For us to be able to instantly retrieve a word at a glance and simply read it, the brain must have previously mapped the graphemes onto the sounds and linked this visual and auditory information to the meaning of the word. This process, which occurs in the brain for each individual word, is called orthographic mapping and results in reading automaticity. Simply put, the more opportunities a pupil has to read or spell words (and orthographically map them), the greater the likelihood that they will be able to retrieve them with automaticity. Studies have shown that the increased intensity of this repetition positively impacts pupil achievement [5].

Repetition is built into phonics programmes, but for many pupils, this is not sufficient. This is where the games in this chapter become a useful addition to classroom practice. They offer pupils the opportunity to learn and cement their knowledge of the relationship between sounds and graphemes, practice reading and spelling words, and work towards automaticity.

Specifically, each of the activities in this chapter focusses on one or more of the key areas of phonics:

- Phonemic awareness – recognising, isolating; and identifying phonemes in spoken words.
- Code knowledge – the relationship between phonemes and graphemes.
- Exploration of the phonemes.
- Learning about the graphemes.
- Key skills – blending and segmenting.

The activities in this chapter can be used at any stage in a pupil's phonics journey, as they can be matched to where they are in a programme. Whether they are just beginning with basic code or are exploring advanced code, where graphemes are made up of multiple letters, pupils will enjoy these activities. Extensions and adaptions for access are available for some activities, as required.

Explanation of phonics terms

Below is an overview of each of the common phonics terms used within the book. The language is simplified to ensure that any adult can complete a phonics activity without specific expertise in teaching phonics.

Automaticity – The ability to rapidly, effortlessly, and accurately recognise or decode words.

Phoneme – The individual sounds that make up spoken words. There are 44 phonemes in the English language.

Grapheme – The written symbols that represent the sounds. Graphemes can be made up of one or more letters to spell a sound.

Blending – The process of combining sounds to make a spoken word.

Segmenting – The process of splitting a spoken word into its component sounds in sequence.

Letter names – The names we give letters as heard in the alphabet. These are generally not used when focussing on phonics, as they are different to the phonemes, and graphemes may be made up of multiple letters.

CVC/CVCC etc. – C is a consonant, V is a vowel

Phonemic awareness – The ability to isolate, identify, and work with the sounds in spoken words.

Activities included in this chapter

Activity	Whole class	Groups	Pairs	Individuals	Extensions	Adaptions
Sound hunt						
Sensory writing						
Board games						
Phonics puzzle						
Treasure hunt						
Physical phonics						
Phonics Jenga						
Reading cups						
Code creator						
Stop the bus!						

Sound hunt

One key aspect of phonemic awareness is the ability to isolate and identify sounds. This activity encourages children to identify the initial sound in spoken words.

Aims

To identify the initial phoneme in spoken words.

Items needed per group

- Paper and pens.
- Objects around the classroom.

Lesson plan 1 – Whole class

- Allocate each pupil a different phoneme. *When pupils are in the early stages of instruction, they may have only worked on a small number of phonemes, so you will need to allocate the same sound to some pupils.*
- Ask pupils to find items that start with the phoneme.
- These should be small objects whose name starts with the phoneme, e.g., /p/ pen, /sh/ shoe, etc.
- Set a timer for the pupils to go and find the objects.
- When the pupils return, ask them to share their "treasure" and compare how many objects they found. Are there some pupils who have lots to share and others who have less? What does this tell us about how common some phonemes are relative to others?

Lesson plan 2 – Pairs/small groups

- Ask each pupil to think of a phoneme.
- The pupils then think of some objects around the classroom that start with that phoneme. They should draw these objects on a piece of paper, keeping their work secret from their peers.
- The pupils then pair up and take it in turns to explore their chosen phonemes.

- Pupil 1 tells pupil 2 what sound they have chosen, and pupil 2 has to look around the classroom and find objects that start with that sound. They draw the objects on a piece of paper.
- Pupils then compare their drawings: Do they match? Did they find more or less items?
- The pupils then swap so pupil 1 becomes the treasure hunter of the phoneme that pupil 1 chose.

Extensions

Option 1 – Ask pupils to write the name of each of the objects that they find and then highlight the grapheme that represents the focus phoneme (this should be when pupils are working at advanced code level). As well as objects, encourage pupils to think about words that can describe the objects, e.g., shiny, rough, or slippery.

Option 2 – Rather than focussing on just the initial phoneme, ask pupils to find objects that contain the target phoneme anywhere in the word.

Adaptions

Option 1 – Provide a table or tray of objects for pupils to look at and choose objects. These should include objects that start with a range of phonemes.

Sensory writing

Learning to form the shapes of letters accurately requires much practice. This activity allows pupils to explore the shapes of different letters using different media. Pupils use their fingers or objects to trace the shapes and "write" the graphemes or words.

Aims

To write letters using a variety of media. To accurately write a specific letter.

Items needed per group

- Sand or flour (in Tupperware or tray).
- Sticks.
- Pebbles.
- Chalk.

Lesson plan 1 – Pairs

- Each pair will need a Tupperware or tray of sand.
- Pupil 1 will choose a phoneme and say it out loud.
- Pupil 2 will then use their finger to write the grapheme in the sand, saying the phoneme at the same time as forming the letter shape(s).
- This could be made more complex by providing graphemes containing multiple letters or phonemes that can be spelt in different ways.

Lesson plan 2 – Pairs

- Pupils will need a selection of pebbles or sticks and a flat surface.
- Pupil 2 will need to close their eyes.
- Pupil 1 will then create a letter using the sticks or pebbles.
- Pupil 1 should carefully hold pupil 2's hand to guide them to the start of the letter.
- Pupil 2 can then feel along the pebbles or sticks to try and identify the letter without looking. They say the phoneme that matches the letter.

Lesson plan 3 – Small groups/pairs

- Pupil 1 will be giving instructions. The other pupils will need a piece of chalk and flat tarmac (if doing this as an outdoor activity) or a pen and paper.
- Pupil 1 should give simple instructions to form a letter or series of letters of their choosing. Encourage the child to think about the specifics of how the letter is formed. They should include information on where on the page to start. They could use upper and lower case letters.
- The other pupils will then listen the instructions and follow what is being said to create the letters. Ask them to try not to predict what the letter or word might be until the instructions are finished.

Adaptions

Option 1 – Give the pupils letter flashcards or an alphabet board for reference to help them choose a letter and guess the phoneme.

Board games

This activity uses simple board games to practice matching phonemes to graphemes and reading. The games can focus on sounds or words matched to the pupils' level. There is also an opportunity for pupils to support each other with reading.

Aims

To identify graphemes or words as part of a game.
To identify words that contain specific graphemes.
To read words and identify their meaning.

Items needed per group

- Tic-tac-toe – make a grid with graphemes in each square.
- Connect 4 – make a grid with seven columns and six rows, each with a grapheme or word, or alternatively use masking tape to write on the counters of a real Connect 4 game.
- Snakes and Ladders – simple board game with words on each square.
- Counters.
- Dice.

Note that printable board game templates are available online and can be edited and printed out. Simply add the graphemes or words into the spaces in the template. When working at the basic code level in the early stages of instruction, letters or words will need to be repeated to fill the board.

Lesson plan 1 – Pairs (tic-tac-toe)

- Played as a typical tic-tac-toe game, with pupils placing counters in the squares.
- When the pupil chooses where to place their counter, they should read the grapheme.
- After reading the grapheme, the pupil should think of a word that starts with that grapheme.
- If they can correctly identify a word, they place their counter on the square. If they cannot identify a word or if they read the grapheme incorrectly, they can choose a different square and try again.

- The game continues until one player wins.

Lesson plan 2 – Pairs (Connect 4)

- Played as a typical Connect 4 game, with pupils placing counters in the squares, however pupils must remember to "drop" their counters to the lowest square available in that column.
- When they choose a square, they should read the matching grapheme or word, as appropriate.
- After saying the phoneme, the pupil should think of a word that starts with the phoneme, or after reading a word they should try and put it into a sentence or explain what it means. If they cannot identify the phoneme or the word, encourage them to ask a peer for support. Their peers might be able to say a word that starts with the phoneme or put the word in a sentence so the pupil can work it out.
- Continue playing the game until one player wins.

Lesson plan 3 – Small groups (Snakes and Ladders)

- The pupils take turns to roll the dice and move their counter.
- Each time they land on a square they read the word.
- When they have read the word, the pupil should try and put the word into a sentence or explain what it means. If they cannot identify the word, encourage them to ask a peer for support. Their peers might be able to say a word that starts with the sound or put the word in a sentence so the pupil can work it out.
- Continue playing the game until one player wins.

Extensions

Option 1 – Ask your pupils to think of words or create sentences in a specific tense. For example, using the past, present, or future tense.

Phonics puzzle

In this activity, pupils plan and make word puzzles. The activity can be matched to the phonics the pupils are working on in class. By asking pupils to include specific graphemes, you can test their recall, knowledge, and application.

Aims

To create a puzzle using their phonics knowledge. To build words using their component graphemes. To read and identify the meaning of words.

Items needed per group

- Cardboard.
- Paper.
- Glue.
- Pens.
- Paperclip.

Lesson plan – Pairs/individuals

- Pupils start by thinking of at least five words and writing them down.
- Encourage them to use different coloured pens to highlight different graphemes in the word.
- On a separate piece of paper, they write each word with a gap between each grapheme.
- They will also need to draw or print out a picture of the word.
- Once they have completed this for all of their chosen words, they glue everything onto a piece of cardboard.
- They then cut out each of the graphemes thinking about what it would look like in a puzzle. They could cut out simple squares or other shapes.
- They will also need to cut out the matching picture.
- The pupils clip together the graphemes and matching pictures for each word.
- Pupils can then swap their puzzles and solve each other's to build and read the words.

Extensions

Option 1 – Encourage the pupils to make their puzzles as instructed but not include any pictures of the words. The pupils will then need to work out what words can be made without an image prompt.

Adaptions

Option 1 – Write a small number 1 in the corner of the card containing each puzzle's first grapheme to give pupils a starting point.

Option 2 – Provide the pupils with a pre-made puzzle that they can put together, or provide them with appropriate words to turn into puzzles.

Treasure hunt

This activity ensures pupils think about their writing and spelling when setting up the hunt and focus on reading accurately when completing their peers' treasure hunts.

Aims

To identify matching lower and upper case letters (1). To read words and relate to their meaning (2). To follow written instructions (2).

Items needed per group

- Pens.
- Small pieces of paper (2).
- Blu Tack (2).

Lesson plan 1 – Small groups/pairs

- Matching lower and upper case letters
- The group is split into two. Each group creates their own treasure hunt. They can then complete their peers' hunt.
- Each group chooses five letters that they can write.
- They write the first letter on a small piece of paper in lower case.
- On a second small piece of paper, they write the upper case of letter 1 and the lower case of letter 2.
- On a third piece they write the upper case of letter 2 and the lower-case of letter 3. And so on.
- On the final piece of paper, they draw the final upper case letter and the treasure!
- Pupils then place their papers, except for paper 1, around the classroom. Make sure the papers are folded so that the upper case letter is visible.
- Pupils then swap paper 1 with the other half of the group.
- Once they have identified the first letter, they look around the classroom for the matching upper case letter.
- Once they have found the upper case letter, they read the next lower case letter and look for the upper case letter, and so on.

- They should continue until they find the treasure! To complete the treasure hunt they must find the letters in order.

Lesson plan 2 – Small groups/pairs

- Matching words and pictures.
- The group is split into two. Each group creates their own treasure hunt. They can then complete their peers' hunts.
- Each group chooses five words that they can write and draw a picture for.
- On a small piece of paper, they write the first word.
- On a second small piece of paper they draw the picture to match word 1 and write word 2.
- On a third piece they draw picture 2 and write word 3. And so on.
- On the final piece of paper they draw the picture and the treasure!
- Pupils then place their papers, except for "word 1", around the classroom. Make sure the papers are folded so that the picture is visible.
- Pupils then swap "word 1" with the other half of the group.
- Once they have read the first word, they look around the classroom for the matching picture.
- Once they have found the picture, they read the next word and look for the matching picture, and so on.
- They should continue until they find the treasure! To complete the treasure hunt they must find the pictures in order.

Adaptions

Option 1 (lesson plan 1) – Provide images matching the letters, e.g., apple for a.

Physical phonics

This activity combines the physical with the cognitive by providing stimulating phonics activities with running, jumping, and throwing activities.

Aims

To work as part of a team to solve problems. To identify sounds or words as part of a game. To identify words that start with specific sounds.

Items needed per group

- Playground.
- Chalk.
- Bean bags.
- Hula hoops.
- Hurdles (if you don't have any, use planks of wood or draw rectangles on the ground).
- Ball.

Lesson plan – Whole class/small groups/pairs/individuals

- Set up five stations around the playground. Pupils can support setting up. Split the class into five groups.
- Each group will need to be allocated to an activity. Give the pupils time to complete each activity before moving them on to the next station.

These activities can be completed independently of the others as a warm-up or filler activity. They are also great practice for individual students.

Activity 1 – The first station is hopscotch. Draw a hopscotch grid on the playground using chalk, but instead of adding numbers in each square, write different graphemes that pupils are focussing on in class. To play, the pupils throw a beanbag onto one of the squares, "hopscotch" to the square, pick up the beanbag, and say the sound. They should continue until they reach the end of the hopscotch. They pass the beanbag on and the next pupil has a go.

Activity 2 – The second station is the long jump. Draw a starting line and a line that they will jump from after a run up. After that, draw a line every 10 cm. To the left of each line, write a word that matches to the phonics the pupils are working on in class. To play, the pupils stand on the start line, run to the jump line, and jump forwards. When they land, their peers should look to see which line they are closest to, and everyone then reads the word on that line. The "jumper" could also put the word into a sentence.

Activity 3 – The third station is the beanbag throw. Draw a standing line for the pupils to stand behind when throwing. Place hula hoops on the ground in front of the standing line. They should be scattered randomly, with some closer and some further away. In each hoop, write a grapheme or word. The pupils throw a beanbag into one of the hoops and say the sound that matches the grapheme or read the word. They can try and think of a word that starts with the sound or put the word into a sentence.

Activity 4 – The fourth station is the hurdles. These can be real obstacles such as planks of wood or they can be lines drawn onto the floor to jump over. Set up a start line and five or six hurdles. At each hurdle write a grapheme. Pupils run and jump over the hurdles, and as they jump over, each says the sound that matches the grapheme.

Activity 5 – The final activity is throw and catch. Pupils will need to be in pairs or small groups for this activity. Individuals could play by throwing the ball against the wall and catching it. Give the pupils a sound that they are learning or have learnt, and ask them to think of words that start with the sound. The challenge is to pass the ball around the group until no one can think of another word. Make it harder by telling pupils they can't hesitate or say umm, urgh, etc.

Phonics Jenga

Jenga is a well-known game that can be used in various ways. This activity uses the Jenga blocks as manipulatives to support blending and reading.

Aims

To read a word using phonics knowledge. To create a word from sound spellings given. To place a word in a sentence using knowledge of its meaning.

Items needed per group

- Jenga blocks.
- Masking tape.
- Felt tip pens.
- Paper (2).

Lesson plan 1 – Small groups/pairs/individuals

- Cut pieces of masking tape just shorter that the length of the Jenga blocks.
- Pupils place a piece of tape onto each block.
- With a felt tip pen, pupils should think of a word they can spell and write it onto the block. Keep going until all of the blocks have a word written on them.
- Build the Jenga tower.
- Pupils take it in turns to remove a block from the tower and read the word.
- They could also try and put the word into a sentence before placing the block on the top of the tower.
- Keep playing until the tower falls down.

Lesson plan 2 – Small groups/pairs

- Cut pieces of masking tape just shorter that the length of the Jenga blocks.
- Place a piece of tape onto each block.
- On each block write a grapheme that they have learnt.
- Build the Jenga tower.

- Pupils take it in turns to remove a block from the tower. They say the sound that matches the grapheme and write it down on their piece of paper.
- The pupil then places the block on the top of the tower.
- Keep playing until the tower falls down.
- When the tower falls, the pupils will have multiple graphemes written on their piece of paper. Using these, they should try and create as many words as they can. If they don't have very many, they can work together to form words using the graphemes from all of their papers.

Extension

Option 1 (lesson plan 1) – When pupils start to pull out the same words or graphemes, challenge them not to repeat the sentences they create.

Option 2 (lesson plan 2) – Challenge the pupils to see who can create the longest word using their graphemes. Pupils can compare their lists of words and lose points for each word that another pupil has written.

Reading cups

In addition to learning to blend and segment, pupils also need to learn how to manipulate sounds or slide them in and out of words. This activity involves moving the cups to change one of the graphemes within the word.

Aims

To create words by changing one of the graphemes.
To blend and read words.

Items needed per group

- Paper cups.
- Craft knife.
- Paper.
- Pens.

Lesson plan 1 – Pairs/individuals

- This activity focusses on changing one sound in a CVC word with the pupil reading the new word that is created.
- By making different sets of cups you can focus on the first, second, or third sound:

First sound e.g., dad-sad-bad-lad-mad,
Second sound e.g., bat-bet-bit-bot-but,
Third sound e.g., pip-pin-pig-pit.

- On the outer cup, write the letters that will not be changed, with a gap for where the change will be made.
- Use a craft knife to cut out a hole in the cup where the change will happen.
- On the inner cup write the letters that will change the word.
- Place the second cup inside the first.
- Pupils can then move the cups around to form different words.
- Encourage them to read the words they create and explain what they mean.

Note that although it is possible to generate nonsense words, try to focus on real words that pupils know the meaning of.

Extensions

Option 1 – Ask the pupil to "build the word" using the cups. Then, tell them what word you want them to change it to. After they have moved the cups, you can check whether they made the correct sound swap. Pupils could complete this in pairs, with one choosing the word and the second moving the cups.

Code creator

This activity highlights the nature of the code as they create their own to spell and read words. Pupils must make sure they have correctly spelt words to ensure their peers are able to accurately read and crack *their* code.

Aims

To appreciate the nature of the alphabetic code. To create a code using phonics knowledge. To crack a code using phonics knowledge.

Items needed per group

- Paper.
- Pen.

Lesson plan 1 – Pairs/individuals

- Each pair/individual thinks of a sentence to write. It is helpful to write it down and then identify all the graphemes.
- On a new piece of paper they write a key to their code by assigning each grapheme a new symbol of their own choosing. This could be different colours, shapes, or "made up" symbols.
- They then code their sentence and write it down.
- Once the pupils have finished they swap with their peers.
- They children crack the code and work out what the sentence is.

Lesson plan 2 – Pairs/individuals

- Each pair/individual chooses a book that matches to the phonics they are working on in class, e.g., their current decodable reader. This will be the key for their book cipher.
- The task is to find words within the book and discover a hidden message.
- To create the message, they start by finding the words in the book.

- For each word, they note the page number, how many lines from the top of the page the word is, and how many words along on the line the target word is. An example is (6,2,3), on page 6, 2 lines down, word 3.
- Pupils will need to write their code on a piece of paper, with each word's code being written in brackets or on a separate line.
- Once the pupils have finished setting out their code, they should swap with their peers and give them the book.
- When their peers have cracked the code, they should read it out to the creators to see if they got it correct.

Extensions

Option 1 – Extend the pupils by asking them to write multiple sentences into their code and ask them to include specific graphemes.

Adaptions

Option 1 (lesson plan 1) – Instead of writing the code with each shape representing a grapheme, have each shape represent a letter in the alphabet.

Option 2 (lesson plan 2) – Give the pupils a code that you have already written using a book that matches to the phonics they are working on in class. Let them follow the code to find the words and write the sentence.

Stop the bus!

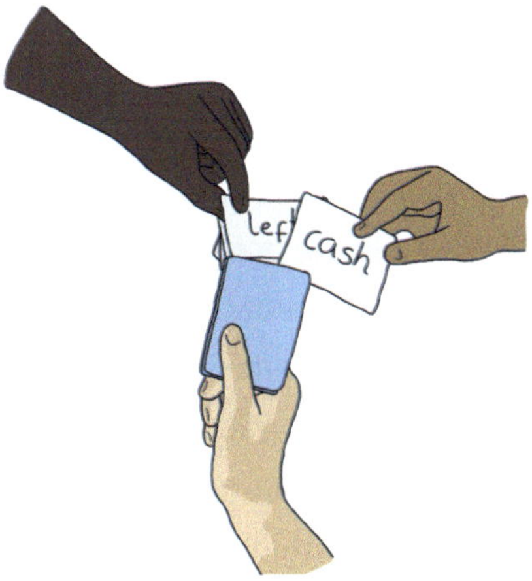

This activity encourages pupils to listen to the phonemes being used, separating the individual sounds and how they are spelt. The games can be quite fast-paced, leaving little time to get distracted, creating a higher engagement level.

Aims

To actively listen to the words being read. To notice specific phonemes. To explore the different graphemes used to make the same phoneme.

Items needed per group

- Book/poem (1).
- Flashcards with words written on with multiple cards of words containing the same phonemes (2) – these could be made by using masking tape on playing cards and then writing on the tape.

Lesson plan 1 – Whole class/small groups/pairs

- Identify one or more phonemes that are included in the book/poem.
- You will need to read the book/poem out loud to the pupils. The task for the pupils is to listen carefully and identify when they hear the specified phonemes.
- When they hear a word containing the phoneme, they should shout out "Stop the bus!".
- Pupils must then identify the word containing the phoneme. See if they can identify if the words through the book have the same grapheme for the phoneme.
- Continue reading until they shout at you to stop again.
- If there is a phoneme that they don't notice, pause the reading and let them know. Go back and read the sentences or phrase again and ask them to try and identify the phoneme.

Lesson plan 2 – Small groups/pairs

- This game is to be played like snap. But instead of looking for matching cards, the pupils are listening out for the same phonemes.

- Split the cards evenly between the players. Each player should hold their cards face down.
- The first pupil turns over their top card, placing it on the table. They should then read out the word.
- The pupils go around the group, each turning over their top card and placing it on the pile then reading out the word.
- If the pupil reads out a word that has a matching phoneme with the card already on the pile, all pupils race to put their hand on the pile and say "snap!".
- The pupil whose hand is first on the pile takes the stack of cards.
- The pupil with the most cards at the end of a time limit, or the last pupil with cards in their hand is the winner of the game.
- Make sure to shuffle the cards before playing again.

Adaptions

Option 1 (lesson plan 1) – Project the book onto the class board so that the pupils can follow along as you read, making it easier to identify the location of phonemes. However, it is important to be aware that most phonemes can be represented by more than one grapheme.

Option 2 (lesson plan 2) – Include images and words on the flashcards to assist with reading comprehension.

Reference list

1. Johnston, R. and Watson, J. 2005. *The effects of synthetic phonics teaching on reading and spelling attainment: A seven year longitudinal study.* Edinburgh: Scottish Executive Central Research Unit.

2. Department for Education, 2023. *The reading framework*, July 2023. Available at https://www.gov.uk/government/publications/the-reading-framework-teaching-the-foundations-of-literacy.

3. Scarborough, H.S., Neuman, S. and Dickinson, D., 2009. Connecting early language and literacy to later reading (dis) abilities: Evidence, theory, and practice. *Approaching Difficulties in Literacy Development: Assessment, Pedagogy and Programmes*, *10*, pp.23–38.

4. Patria, L., 2023, June. Improving students 'motivation in learning phonics through games. In *Proceedings of the 2nd International Conference on Advances in Humanities, Education and Language, ICEL 2022, 7–8 November 2022, Malang, Indonesia*.

5. Dilgard, C., Hodges, T.S. and Coleman, J., 2022. Phonics instruction in early literacy: Examining professional learning, instructional resources, and intervention intensity. *Reading Psychology*, *43*(8), pp.541–575.

Chapter 5
NUMERACY

Maths covers a wide range of topics, from the four operations to understanding a range of measures and the language required to explain each area. Numeracy is the extension of this into real-world situations and the ability to apply maths to make the most appropriate decisions. The activities in this chapter focus on the basic concepts in math by centring them in games and tasks that require critical thinking. The activities described within the chapter adhere to and enrich the prescribed national standards, covering a range of topics from basic arithmetic operations to shapes, measures, and mathematical reasoning.

A solid foundation in mathematics is crucial for understanding complex concepts and solving challenging problems. This foundation is often established and reinforced through repetition. Repetition in maths practice helps memorise key formulas, understand fundamental principles deeply, and develop problem-solving skills. Studies in cognitive and educational psychology demonstrate how superior long-term learning is developed through repeated encounters with material over time compared with repetitions grouped together [1]. The activities in this chapter can be used as whole lessons, as starters or as time fillers at any point in a pupil's journey, supporting the required repetition in pupils' numeracy development.

One technique the activities take advantage of is the gamification of numeracy tasks to create a more engaging way to understand mathematical concepts and reduce the boredom of repeated topics. Through games, students can practice problem-solving skills, build a deeper understanding of mathematical principles, and develop a positive attitude towards maths. Gamification has also been used as a way to relate concepts learnt in maths to everyday life [2]. This interactive approach to learning not only makes maths more accessible but also encourages participation, collaboration, and competition among students, leading to improved mathematical fluency and confidence.

Moreover, the numeracy chapter encourages the use of manipulatives in the main activities and supports pupils through adaptations. Manipulatives are useful in visualising sums and serve as an invaluable aid in making abstract concepts more concrete. They allow

DOI: 10.4324/9781003515234-6

students to physically manipulate and thus better understand mathematical operations, improving pupil engagement and problem-solving abilities [3]. By providing a visual and tactile experience, manipulatives help foster a deeper comprehension of sums, encouraging learners to engage more fully with mathematical processes.

As previously mentioned, one of the benefits of gamification and manipulatives is the improvement in positive engagement among pupils. Employing a variety of teaching methods to support pupils' learning can help every student feel capable and confident in their maths abilities. Recognising and celebrating progress, no matter how small, will further encourage a positive outlook towards maths, turning it from a subject of dread to one of curiosity and interest.

In exploring ways to enhance educational inclusivity, it becomes vital to examine the role of equity in maths education. This involves considering how various elements, such as socioeconomic factors, gender, and racial biases, significantly influence students' access to quality maths education and their respective attitudes towards the subject. By addressing these issues, we can work towards developing strategies that ensure a more equitable and inclusive approach to maths education, making it accessible and engaging for all students regardless of their background.

Through a blend of gamification, the use of manipulatives, and structured activities aligned with national standards, the chapter equips teachers with tools to make maths both accessible and engaging. By prioritising repetition, critical thinking, and a versatile approach to teaching, it lays down a pathway for students to achieve mathematical fluency and confidence. Moreover, the focus on equity in maths education highlights the importance of addressing broader societal issues within the classroom, ensuring every child has the opportunity to succeed in maths. With these approaches, numeracy becomes a world to be explored and understood, promising a positive impact on pupils' educational journeys and beyond.

Progress in line with the National Curriculum [4]

KS1 – *Confidence and mental fluency with whole numbers, counting and place value. Recognise, describe, draw, compare and sort different shapes. Use a range of measures to describe and measure quantities such as length, mass, volume, time and money. Know number bonds to 20, multiplication and division.*

LKS2 – *Increasing fluency with whole numbers and the four operations, including number facts and place value. Develop efficient written and mental methods and perform accurate calculations with increasingly large numbers. Develop ability to solve a range of problems including with simple fractions and decimal place value. Develop mathematical reasoning to analyse shapes and their properties. Use measuring instruments with accuracy and make connections between measure and number. Memorise their multiplication tables up to and including the 12-multiplication table.*

UKS2 – *Extend understanding of number system and place value to include larger integers. Develop connections between multiplication and division with fractions, decimals, percentages and ratio. Solve wider range of problems including complex properties of numbers and arithmetic using efficient written and mental methods of calculation. Introduction to the language of algebra to solve a variety of problems. Development in geometry and measures, classify increasingly complex geometric properties and learn appropriate language. Be fluent in written methods of all four operations including long multiplication and division, working with fractions, decimals and percentages.*

Activities included in this chapter

Activity	**Whole class**	**Groups**	**Pairs**	**Individuals**	**Extensions**	**Adaptions**
Bounce to multiply						
Number bodies						
Number fact bingo						
Picture this						
Value blocks						
Division drive						
Playdough pizza						
Board game maker						
Big or small?						
101 points						

Bounce to multiply

Times tables are a key part of the maths curriculum, providing a useful building block for future learning; however, they can become repetitive and boring to learn. These activities help engage pupils in times tables with physical activity.

Aims

To practice multiplication. To count forwards and backwards. Understand multiplication as repeated addition.

Items needed per groupp

- 200 square (1).
- Counters (1).
- 2 x 12-sided dice (1) – For young pupils, use one 12-sided dice and a second six-sided dice with masking tape and a pen to change the numbers to cover the times tables currently being learnt.
- Chalk (2).
- Playground (2).
- Stopwatch (2).
- Pen and paper (to mark scores).

Lesson plan 1 – Small groups/pairs

- Lay the 200 square on the table between the pupils. Each pupil will need a counter.
- The first pupil rolls the dice and multiplies the numbers together.
- They then place their counter on the box containing that number.
- The pupils should take it in turns to roll the dice. They may have multiple counters on one box until the next roll.
- Continue for a set amount of time or keep rolling until one pupil has jumped onto all 12 boxes of one times table. This could be recorded on a separate piece of paper, or pupils could have a perfect square to mark off where they have landed.

Lesson plan 2 – Small groups/pairs

- Draw 20 bubbles on the ground. Pupils will need to be able to jump between the bubbles.
- In each bubble, write the numbers included in the times table. Don't write them in order.
- In the remaining bubbles, write numbers that are close to those in the times table.
- Pupil A starts on the first number of the times table.
- Pupil B will need to hold the stopwatch.
- On pupil B's signal, pupil A should jump through the bubbles following the times table. Other pupils can follow to check if they are accurate. Pupil B should time pupil A.
- Pupils can then swap, and each have a go at jumping the times table to see who can complete it the fastest.
- It will be harder for the first pupil, as the others can copy what they have done. Try with different times tables and let a different pupil start.

Adaptions

Option 1 (lesson plan 1) – Use only one dice and choose a specific times table. Roll the dice and multiple the number on the dice by the chosen times table number. For example, for the 5 times tables, you roll a 6, you multiply 5 x 6, you move your counter to 30.

Option 2 (lesson plan 2) – Write the numbers 1–10 or 1–20 in bubbles and have one pupil shout out a number. The other pupil can then run and stand on it. Pupils can take it in turns to find numbers. Or give instructions like 6 and 1 more (pupil runs to stand on 7). Pupils can also jump on each of the numbers in order, forwards or backwards.

Number bodies

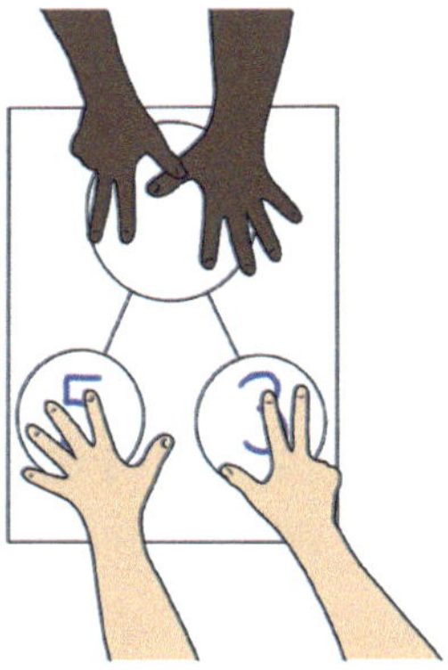

Addition and subtraction are key building blocks for the development of children's maths skills. As the sums are inverse operations of each other, the same activities can be used to practice both skills. The physicality of this activity gets pupils up and out of their seats while providing physical graphics to represent the problem.

Aims

To communicate effectively to work as part of a team. To complete additions and subtractions using whole numbers.

Items needed per group

- Outdoor space.
- Chalk.

Lesson plan – Whole class

- Draw a large set of number bond circles on the ground in chalk, with the whole at the top, linked with lines to two parts below. The circles will need to be big enough for multiple children to stand in them.
- The activity can be used to complete additions or subtractions.
- For addition, tell pupils how many need to stand in each of the "part" circles.
- Then ask the rest of the pupils to calculate how many of them need to stand in the "whole" circle.
- Ask pupils to say the sum out loud, for example, "5 add 5 equals 10".
- For subtraction, tell pupils the whole and encourage that many pupils to stand in the "whole" circle.
- Then tell pupils the amount to subtract. That number of pupils then stands in one of the "part" circles.
- The rest of the pupils work out how many will be left, and that number of pupils then goes and stands in the second "part" circle.
- Ask pupils to say the sum out loud, for example, "10 minus 5 equals 5".

- When completing larger number facts, the pupils standing in the "whole" circle may need to move into the two "part" circles, as the number of each of the circles added together is larger than the number of pupils in the class.
- One pupil could take on the role of giving the instructions to the rest of the class to complete a sum independently.

KS1 – Number bonds to 20 using pupils to represent the numbers. For example, five pupils in one circle and six pupils in the second circle. The rest of the pupils make up the nine for the whole. When working towards higher numbers, you may need to represent the numbers using legs, so each pupil represents two.

KS2 – Addition using numbers larger than 20 can be done by representing each number with a finger. Pupils can stand around the outside of the circle and place the correct number of fingers into the circle.

Extensions

Option 1 – Give pupils a time limit to complete each sum. Encourage them to communicate clearly to complete each sum within the time limit.

Adaptions

Option 1 – Write the numbers that make up the original sum in the two relevant circles. Pupils can then check the numbers before adding themselves to the sum and use them as reference in their calculations.

Number fact bingo

Bingo is a simple game that can be used in lots of ways. This version requires pupils to solve sums before they mark off the numbers on their bingo card. By changing the questions, pupils can be tested at various levels, making it accessible at all levels. It also gives pupils the opportunity to practice mental maths.

Aims

To practice mental maths. To complete number facts up to and including 20 or 100. To complete multiplication and division of numbers within known times tables.

Items needed per group

- Bingo cards.
- Pen.

Note: You will need to make your own bingo cards for KS1 to limit the numbers to the sums they are able to complete.

Lesson plan 1 – Whole class/pairs/individuals

- Each pupil or pair will need a bingo card and a pen.
- You, the bingo master, will need a 100 square to keep track of the numbers called.
- Choose a random number; instead of saying the number out loud, give a sum where the number is the answer.

For example, 4 x 10 (= 40), 12 ÷ 3 (= 4), 53 + 25 (= 78), 16 – 4 (= 12).

- Only ask questions within the pupils' capability.
- Leave time after each sum for pupils to work out the answer and then check their bingo cards.
- Each time, the pupils cross off a number from their bingo card.
- Pupils can shout "bingo!" when they get a row or column and a full house!

KS1 – Number facts up to 20, addition and subtraction. Multiplication and division of times tables that are known.

KS2 – Number facts up to 100, addition and subtraction. Multiplication and division of times tables up to 12.

Extensions

Option 1 – Give sums outside of those they are familiar with, for example, multiplication and division of numbers with answers up to 100, not stopping at 12 x 12, such as 2 x 34 (= 68).

Adaptions

Option 1 – Give pupils a laminated number line or 100 square, including the numbers that are used in the questions. Using a whiteboard pen, they can mark off the numbers as they complete the sums; this can then be rubbed out before the next question.

Option 2 – Limit to one of the four operations, for example only including addition questions.

Picture this

This activity uses squared paper to guide pupils in creating images. For younger pupils, they will focus on drawing with the squares and learning how to mirror an image. Older pupils will focus on creating an image and then writing coordinates to guide their peers to create the same.

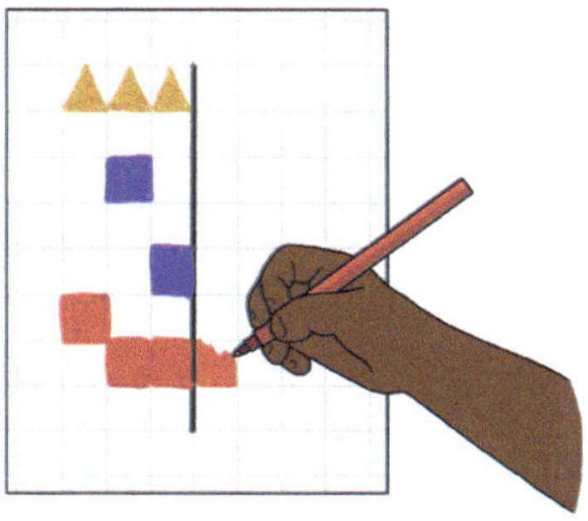

Aims

To create a mirror image (1). To create an image and translate it into coordinates (2). To follow coordinates to create an image (2).

Items needed per group

- Squared paper.
- Pencil.
- Coloured pens.

Lesson plan 1 (KS1) – Small groups/pairs

- On a piece of squared paper, pupils will need to draw a line down the centre in one direction.
- On one side of the line, pupils should create a drawing by colouring in a variety of squares. They can completely fill each square and half fill the squares to create their image.
- Pupils will then need to swap with a peer.
- They then have to copy the pattern drawn as if a mirror is placed down the centre line.

Lesson plan 2 (KS2) – Small groups/pairs/individuals

- Draw a grid with an x- and y-axis on a piece of squared paper. Older pupils can extend their grid to include up to four quadrants.
- Mark the points along each axis using whole numbers.
- Each pupil should create two grids or draw one and then photocopy it before continuing.
- Using the grid, pupils should draw a simple picture made up of a variety of shapes. They will need to create a dot-to-dot style drawing so it can be recreated using coordinates.

- The pupils will write the coordinates needed to recreate their image on the second piece of paper with the blank grid.
- Make sure to write the coordinates in the order they should be connected together. To create multiple lines or shapes, pupils can write sections of the drawing as separate lines of coordinates.
- Pupils can then swap their blank grid and coordinates with a peer who will complete the drawing.

Extensions

Option 1 (lesson plan 1) – Draw a line across the centre of the page, both horizontally and vertically. Pupils can then draw their pattern in one quadrant; the others can also try to repeat the pattern diagonally from the original.

Option 2 (lesson plan 2) – Limit the pupils to only using specific shapes to create a recognisable image. For example, they can only use triangles to draw a robot. They will need to think carefully about how they write the coordinates so their peers can recreate the image accurately.

Adaptions

Option 1 (lesson plan 1) – Provide pupils with a half-completed drawing to mirror.

Option 2 (lesson plan 2) – Provide pupils with a list of coordinates that make an image.

Value blocks

This activity uses the concept of place value and adds a physical and visual element. Using the coloured blocks, pupils can visualise each of the numbers and use them as manipulatives to answer questions.

Aims

To recognise the value of a digit based on its location within a number. Read and write numbers up to the relevant value. To create numbers by representing each value with blocks.

Items needed per group

- Coloured blocks or Lego, one colour for each place value – on the side of each block, write the value; this can be done with a marker pen or masking tape and a pen.
- Pens.
- Pencil.

Lesson plan 1 – Pairs/individuals

- Create a table showing which colour represents each of the place values. Put the colours and place values across the top of the table, including a decimal point if appropriate. Draw the table in pen.
- In the second row, pupils can write the number, placing each value in the correct column. This will help them identify how many of each block they need. Write the numbers in pencil so they can be rubbed out and changed. Or add multiple rows and each new number is written in a new row.
- Pupil A starts by writing a number in the table.
- Pupil B takes the blocks and creates the number, with one block of each colour representing one in that place value. For example, 625 would be six red blocks, two orange blocks, and five yellow blocks.
- The pupils can then swap roles.
- The activity can also be done in reverse. Pupil A uses the blocks to create a number.
- Pupil B then writes the correct number in the table.

- To make it harder, pupils should write the number on a blank piece of paper without using the table as a guide.

KS1 – Recognise place value in two-digit numbers (tens, ones).

LKS2 – Recognise place value in three- and four-digit numbers (thousands, hundreds, tens, ones).

UKS2 – Recognise place value of less than 1 (tenths, hundredths, thousandths). Determine values up to at least 1,000,000.

Extensions

Option 1 – Instead of giving pupil B a number, pupil A can write a sum and then ask pupil B to answer the sum using the blocks.

Option 2 (UKS2) – Create addition, subtraction, multiplication and division sums using the blocks. Once the pupils are confident in completing sums using the blocks, they can try writing the sums without the support of the blocks.

Adaptions

Option 1 – Working on whole numbers up to 20, pupils can represent every "one" with a block. For example, 12 would be ten orange blocks and two yellow blocks rather than one orange block and two yellow blocks.

Division drive

Division is often seen as the hardest of the four operations, and depending on the numbers being used, many different methods are taught. However, across all of the methods, the understanding of multiplication tables and the ability to half a number is important. This activity encourages pupils to complete division using their knowledge of times tables. This activity can also be changed to focus on one of the other operations.

Aims

To mentally divide whole numbers. To use knowledge of times tables when dividing.

Items needed per group

- Toy cars/counters.
- Grid on A3 paper or chalk on table/playground. Ten squares long, width dependant on number of pupils involved (1).
- Pencils/chalk (1).
- Lists of 10 division sums for each pupil (1).

Lesson plan 1 – Small groups/pairs

- Set up the grid with each pupil choosing a car that stands at the start line.
- Each pupil will need a list of ten sums that involve the times tables at their level. The sums should be different for each pupil.
- On "go", the pupils work through the sums on their sheet. Each time they finish a sum, they write the answer in the square and move their car forward.
- Pupils should continue to see who can finish first and then support their peers in completing the course.

Pupils can have sums of differing difficulties and still play against each other to ensure they are working on what is relevant to them. This also evens out the playing field, ensuring that those who are more confident are still challenged and those who struggle with division are able to compete.

Extensions

Option 1 – Add sums that include halving and quartering larger numbers. These could be written as _ ÷ 2 and _ ÷ 4 or ½ of _ and ¼ of _.

Option 2 – Add in sums that create a whole number and remainder. For example, 21 ÷ 5 = 4 r1. Encourage pupils to think about how many times the smaller number fits in the larger number and then count how many is left.

Adaptions

Option 1 – Start with a multiplication question, and follow it with one of the inverse divisions. For example, 4 x 5 = 20, then 20 ÷ 5 = 4.

Playdough pizza

Fractions can be difficult to understand; however, visualising the numerator and denominator using physical manipulatives can support this comprehension. Pizza, cut into equal pieces, is the perfect tool for the task.

Aims

To create a visualisation of a simple fraction. To write a simple fraction.

Items needed per group

- Playdough/salt dough.
- Rolling pin.
- Butter knife.
- Whiteboards and pens.

Lesson plan 1 – Pairs/individuals

- Each pair/individual will need to start by creating a pizza with the playdough. The best way to do this is by rolling the playdough into a ball and then using the rolling pin to flatten it out in multiple directions.
- You should then give the pupils a fraction.
- Pupils can write the fraction on their whiteboard as a reminder. The whiteboard can also be used to work out how to cut their pizza.
- Pupils should use the knife to cut the pizza into the number specified by the denominator.
- They should then remove pieces until the number of slices left represents the numerator.

Option 1 – Pupil A should name a fraction, and then pupil B should try to create the corresponding pizza. Pupils can then swap roles. To support pupils, write a variety of fractions on the board for them to choose from.

Option 2 – Pupil A should create a pizza, and then pupil B should try to write the fraction. Pupils can then swap roles. To support pupils, write a variety of fractions on the board for them to choose from.

Option 3 – Give pupils an improper fraction to create into multiple pizzas. First, they should create the number of pizzas needed and then cut them into the correct amount as signified by the denominator. They will then need to remove any extra slices so the total number of slices across all of the pizzas matches the numerator. Pupils can then write the improper fraction as a mixed number.

Extensions

Option 1 – Give pupils fractions that have not yet been simplified. They can use the playdough to work out the simplification or work out what the simplified fraction is before and then represent it in playdough.

Adaptions

Option 1 – Instead of starting with a circular pizza shape, pupils can roll the playdough into rectangular shapes to create a bar model.

Board game maker

This activity gives pupils some freedom to set questions for their peers and use design elements to create a game for their classmates. While creating a board game, pupils think about questions and how they might answer them; by swapping games with their peers, they have to spend time thinking about the new questions and their answers, giving them more practice.

Aims

To think of appropriate questions using the four operations. To create a board game for your peers. To answer questions from the four operations.

Items needed per group

- A3 paper.
- Coloured pens/pencils.
- Dice.
- Counters.

Lesson plan – Whole class/small groups/pairs

- Each group will need a piece of paper and some pens to create a maths board game.
- Start by drawing a simple track twisting around the page. The track should then be split into squares.
- Label a start and finish at each end of the track to create an a-to-b counter game.
- In some of the squares, pupils can add directions like "Move forward two steps" or "Oh no, fall back five steps".
- On the rest of the squares, pupils should add simple sums which include all four operations.
- Encourage them to include some easier questions and some that require more thinking.
- When every square is filled, pupils can colour in the squares and add decorations to the background of their board game. They could also think of a name for their game and write it on the paper.
- When the games are finished, pupils should swap games with one of their peer groups.

- Each pupil will need to choose a counter. They will then take it in turns rolling the dice.
- The pupil that rolls the dice will then move their counter forward the matching number of steps.
- They then need to answer the question on the square where they land. Their peers should judge if they are correct.
- If they do not get the answer correct, they can try again and work with their peers to answer the question OR move back the counter to where they were at the beginning of their turn.
- Continue until one pupil finishes the course. They are the winner of the game. Pupils can stop there or continue until all pupils reach the finish.
- The groups may want to continue to rotate games until they have played each group's game.

Extensions

Option 1 – Give pupils specifics that they must include for the sums. For example, they must create at least four division questions, or all addition questions must include two 2-digit numbers.

Adaptions

Option 1 – Pre-make the board game with simple questions within the capabilities of the pupils.

Option 2 – Provide pupils with blocks or other manipulatives and number lines or number squares that they can use to work out the answers to the questions.

Big or small?

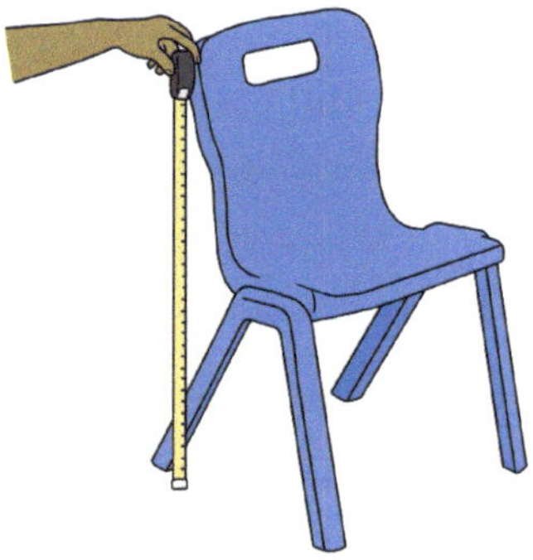

This activity encourages pupils to compare objects using knowledge of measurement. Ordering objects from biggest to smallest is a simple task introduced to young children. It can then be extended to involve measuring the length, height, and width of objects, as well as circumference and capacity.

Aims

To use a ruler or tape measure to record the length of an object. To use scales to weigh an object.

Items needed per group

- Scales (1).
- Ruler/tape measure (1).
- Paper and pen (1).
- Measuring jug (2).
- Cups/jars/bottles of different shapes and sizes (2).
- Access to water (2).

Lesson plan 1 – Small groups/pairs/individuals

- Each pupil will need to search the classroom and choose a random object.
- Each pupil will need to draw a basic image of the object they have chosen on a piece of paper.
- They should then measure the object. This could include height, length, and width. This can be written on the drawing.
- They can then weigh the object and write that down.
- Pupils can compare their objects using the measurements they have taken. If working independently, each pupil should find multiple objects to measure.

Questions can be asked at an appropriate level for the pupils.

Which object is the longest or shortest? Which object is the heaviest or lightest? Which object has the largest or smallest diameter? Can they order five objects using one measurement, such as length?

Lesson plan 2 – Small groups/pairs/individuals

- Provide pupils with a variety of containers that can hold water.
- Pupils should start by guessing which container they think can hold the most water. They should then order the containers to make their predictions, take a photo of them, label them with masking tape and a pen, or draw them.
- The pupils should then fill each container to the top and then use the measuring jug to measure the amount of liquid.
- The pupils should order the containers from the container that can hold the least to the most water.
- They can compare their results with the predictions they made.

Adaptions

Option 1 – Give pupils objects to arrange by size; it will be easier if all of the objects are the same but different sizes. For example, a variety of blocks, pencils, or straws cut to different lengths. Once they have organised the objects, they can measure each of the items.

101 points

The aim of the game is to reach 101 points. Lesson plan 1 reminds pupils of their knowledge of place value and encourages them to think about how their choices might be affected by future dice rolls. Lesson plan 2 involves taking time to work through different options and a variety of different sums before deciding which has the most successful outcome.

Aims

To show workings when completing a sum. To complete sums that include one of the four operations.

Items needed per group

- Dice.
- Pen and paper or whiteboard.

Lesson plan 1 – Whole class/ small groups/pairs/individuals

- Each child will need to draw a table with two columns and six rows. The left column represents tens, and the right column represents ones.
- The teacher rolls the dice.
- Pupils then write the number in the top row, choosing whether it will be in the tens or ones column.
- Roll the dice a second time, and the pupils write the number in the second row.
- Continue until the dice has been rolled six times.
- Pupils add a zero in each of the empty ones cells.
- Pupils should then add all of the digits together.
- The winner is the pupil whose number is closest to 101. Pupils can then work out how far from 101 their number is and think how they might change their strategy when playing again.

Lesson plan 2 – Whole class/ small groups/pairs/individuals

- Roll the dice six times and write each of the numbers on the board for the class or a piece of paper.
- Pupils can work together or alone to work out how to use the six numbers to reach 101.
- They can use any of the four operations: Addition, subtraction, multiplication, or division.
- Give pupils a set amount of time to complete the task.
- Compare answers to see whose answer is closest to 101.

Extensions

Option 1 – After pupils have had a few attempts, change the target number and repeat the activity.

Adaptions

Option 1 (lesson plan 2) – Reduce the target number and only allow addition and subtraction. You can then provide pupils with manipulative objects that they can use to represent the numbers rolled.

Reference List

1. Kang, S.H., 2016. Spaced repetition promotes efficient and effective learning: Policy implications for instruction. *Policy Insights from the Behavioral and Brain Sciences*, *3*(1), pp.12–19.

2. Sakai, K. and Shiota, S., 2016. A practical study of mathematics education using gamification. *International Association for Development of the Information Society.* https://eric.ed.gov/?id=ED571606

3. Monte, J., 2021. An exploration of manipulatives in math education. Bridgewate State University.

4. National curriculum in England: mathematics programmes of study – key stages 1 and 2. Available at https://www.gov.uk/government/publications/national-curriculum-in-england-mathematics-programmes-of-study/national-curriculum-in-england-mathematics-programmes-of-study

Chapter 6
SCIENCE

This chapter allows young scientists to carry out investigations and ask their own "What if...?" questions. It encourages enquiry following a scientific framework with exciting activities and those requiring more time and thought. Each investigation provides a starting point for pupils to change or customise the method or ingredients, leading to comparisons between results. Not only can pupils experience each activity first-hand, but using available technology, experiments can be enhanced through videos, such as slow-motion explosions or time lapses of plants growing.

The field of science education is always evolving, with various individuals championing it for a range of reasons. Some advocate for its significance as a fundamental pillar for future scientific breakthroughs, believing it equips individuals with the vital skills required for forthcoming employment prospects. Additionally, it's seen as aligning with political objectives aimed towards fostering economic growth [1]. This multifaceted support emphasises the role of science education not just in individual development but also in societal progress, hinting at its potential to address global challenges through innovation and informed policymaking. This need for innovation and informed policy making is a particularly prevalent issue with the continued fight against climate change and food distribution, challenges that are felt globally.

Encouraging children's curiosity through science is essential and can be integrated across various subjects in the curriculum, fostering a holistic and self-led approach to learning. Some of this can be supported through the gamification of the scientific process, which includes utilising competition and leaderboards, collaborating for joint progression, storytelling, and puzzles. Gamification of science has been shown to boost student motivation and engagement. Improvements have also been shown in learning outcomes, with gamification supporting pupils in a field that often presents negative emotions and difficulties in understanding [2].

One important aspect of science is the ability to follow instructions, a skill that is developed in the communication chapter. This skill is not only crucial during adolescence and adulthood but also fundamental in many areas of life. In the context of conducting science experiments,

DOI: 10.4324/9781003515234-7

accurately following instructions can mean the difference between achieving meaningful results or facing the disappointment of a failed experiment. Instructions can be conveyed in various forms: Verbally, through illustrations or photos, or as written text. This flexibility ensures that individuals with different learning access needs can still effectively understand and apply the instructions given.

Throughout this chapter, we explore diverse methods for engaging with and comprehending instructions. For instance, each experiment could be introduced to the class through a live demonstration, allowing students to grasp the procedure and replicate it visually. Alternatively, experiments can be described through detailed written documents or illustrated sets of instructions. This can be a challenge to some and a support to others. This approach not only reinforces the importance of following instructions but also emphasises the value of clear communication and the versatility required to convey or understand instructions across different mediums.

Progress in line with the National Curriculum [3]

KS1 – *Asking simple questions. Observing experiments and suggesting answers to questions. Recording data.*

Pupils in KS1 can participate in experiments by following the instructions, asking questions, and answering based on what they can see. Data can be recorded in video and photo formats to support writing.

LKS2 – *Follow practical scientific methods, asking relevant questions and using scientific enquiry to answer them. Setting up experiments and making systematic observations. Recording data and reporting on findings. Identifying similarities or changes in processes and using straightforward scientific evidence to answer questions and support findings.*

Pupils in LKS2 can begin to think more in-depth about the experiment and how it happens. Encourage them to record their data, such as the materials used or the height of the explosion. Use the extensions to guide discussions on how the experiment could be changed.

UKS2 – *Plan experiments, including control variables. Taking accurate measurements and recording data and results using scientific diagrams. Using test results to make predictions of further tests. Presenting findings with conclusions and explanations of results. Identifying scientific evidence that supports or refutes ideas or arguments.*

Pupils in UKS2 should be able to complete the experiments confidently, recording important data and finding ways to present the data, such as a bar graph showing the different heights of explosions depending on the ingredients used. They can also use the extensions to further their thinking and think of their own independent variables.

Layout of this chapter

The activities in this chapter are laid out slightly differently to include the important elements of a science experiment.

1. A question: What will happen when...?
2. An answer (hypothesis): I think that...
3. You will need: A list of ingredients and tools.
4. The experiment: A step-by-step of how to complete the experiment.
5. Lesson plan: Ideas on how pupils can perform the experiment.
6. The results: The science of the experiment explained. Do the results match your hypothesis?
7. Extension: Try again but change something. Change one element of the experiment and measure its effect on the final result, keeping everything else the same.

Note

Group sizes are not specifically included in this chapter, as all experiments can be completed as a demonstration to the whole class and then completed by small groups, pairs, or individuals.

Activities included in this chapter

Activity	Whole class	Groups	Pairs	Individuals	Extensions	Adaptions
Cola volcano						
Plant environments						
Chain reaction						
Oobleck						
Storm in a glass						
Dancing raisins						
Egg drop						
Bottle xylophone						
Bridge building						
Balloon cars						

Cola volcano

One of the parts of science that attracts young minds is explosions – big reactions that are visible and quantifiable. Introducing science with excitement encourages children to be curious and further explore. This experiment can get messy but it's definitely worth it!

Question: What will happen if Mentos are added to a bottle of Coke?

Hypothesis: The Mentos and Coke will react, creating an explosion of bubbles.

Items needed per group

- 2 litre bottle of Diet Coke.
- Packet of mentos.
- Outdoor space or large tray (to contain exploded cola).
- Paper and pens/pencils.

The experiment

- Place the bottle in the tray or outdoor space. Open the bottle.
- Open the packet of Mentos and hold a few in your hand.
- Count down from 10.
- When you reach 0, add the Mentos to the Coke bottle and watch what happens!

Lesson plan

- Run the experiment as a presentation to the class or give each group/pair the ingredients to complete themselves.
- Before starting, ask each pupil to think about what will happen. Write the suggestions down on the board.
- Complete the count down together, and on 0 drop the mentos in the bottle.
- Ask pupils to think about a detail they noticed. What colour was the froth? How quickly did it happen?

- The next part can be done on the board as a whole class, or pupils can complete it independently.
- Ask pupils to draw and label each step of the experiment clearly, creating instructions for someone else to follow.
- They will also need to write a list of ingredients and tools that someone will need to complete the experiment.

The results

The fizz of carbonated drinks like Diet Coke comes from carbon dioxide. The gas tries to escape and forms bubbles around any irregular surface; this is called a nucleation site. Mentos have an irregular surface. If looked at through a microscope, you can see that they are not as smooth as they appear. When they are added to Coke, the dissolved gas pushes the liquid out of the container in the form of bubbles. The Mentos are simply the catalyst releasing the gas from the bottle.

Extensions (try again but change something)

Option 1 – Crush the Mentos before adding them to the bottle of coke.

Option 2 – Try using a different fizzy pop such as 7up or test the difference between regular and Diet Coke. This could be done by different groups or individuals and then bringing pupils together at the end to compare results.

Adaptions

Option 1 – Create a visual step-by-step and illustrated descriptions of different sections of the process. Ask pupils to order the steps and add descriptions to the appropriate areas, for example, putting "frothy" next to the explosion step.

Plant environments

Plants are an essential resource; we use them for food and medicine, they produce the air we breathe and can be used as building materials. Other living things also need plants to live, so learning how they stay alive is essential.

Question: What do plants need to grow?

Hypothesis: Plants need water, light, and soil to grow.

Items needed per group

- Six plant pots.
- Pea seeds.
- Soil or compost.
- Ruler.
- Paper and pen for notes.

The experiment

- There are multiple ways this experiment can be carried out depending on the variable being tested.
- WATER – Plant a couple of pea seeds in soil in each of the pots. Place all of the pots on a windowsill with plenty of sunlight. Label one pot [no water], label the second [water every three days], and label the third [water every day].
- LIGHT – Plant a couple of pea seeds in soil in each of the pots. The pots will need to be put in three different locations, one on the windowsill, one at the opposite end of the room to the window, and one in a cupboard with no light. All of the seeds should be watered regularly.
- SOIL – Fill one pot completely and plant the seeds, put some soil in the second pot and place the seeds on top, and put no soil in the third pot. All of the pots should be placed on a windowsill with plenty of sunlight and watered regularly.

Lesson plan

- Talk about what a plant needs to grow; answers might include space, the right temperature, sunlight, water, air, nutrients/soil, and time.

- Split pupils into three groups/pairs/individuals. A whole class could have multiple groups completing the same experiment.
- Each group should be assigned one of the three key things needed – water, light, or soil.
- Ask pupils to think about three different scenarios to place some seeds in to test the hypothesis that the plant needs their assigned element. Ideas for these are highlighted above within the experiment section.
- Each group will need to set up and label their experiment.
- Over the next week, the pupils will need to continue to monitor their plants and, when relevant, water them.
- Each day they can spend five minutes checking their plants. They could create a table with a column for each plant and a row for each day. Note the height of the plant and any other features that are interesting, such as the colour.
- After one week, the pupils can look at their plants and their notes. They will be able to make statements about what had the most effect on the plants by comparing their results to others who completed the other experiments.

The results

Plants need water, soil, and sunlight to grow. The plants that were deprived completely of one element will either not grow at all or grow very slowly and without their full features.

Extensions

Option 1 – The experiment can also be conducted by changing the amount of space the plant has to grow and the temperature of the air.

Chain reaction

A chain reaction is a series of events that occur in succession due to the impact of the event before. Chain reactions are a great way to learn about kinetic energy, gravity, and friction, and they also engage children in creative thinking. This activity requires lots of patience to wait until you have finished building before knocking it down!

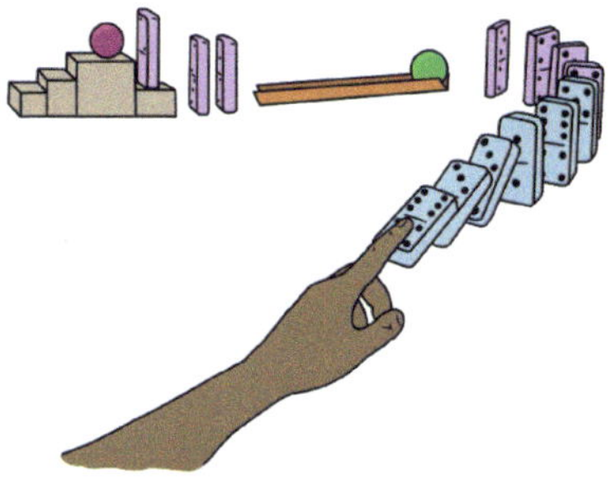

Question: What will happen when one object in a line is knocked down?

Hypothesis: The first object will knock down the second and so on, creating a chain reaction.

Items needed per group

- Stopwatch.
- Camera.
- Dominoes.
- Books.
- Ball.
- Marbles.
- Wooden planks and blocks.
- Cardboard.

The experiment

- Start by showing the pupils a chain reaction of dominoes. Talk about how each domino knocks down the next one until they have all fallen down.
- Show the pupils different variations with the dominos stacked close together and further apart.
- Add a ball at the beginning and roll it into the row of dominoes to start the reaction. You could set up a mini ramp for the ball to roll down.
- Allow pupils to experiment with different materials.

Lesson plan – Small groups/pairs/individuals

- Each group will need access to a variety of materials to build with.

- Set a length for each group to cover with their chain.
- Let them experiment with different materials. Encourage them to try and add more than one material to their chain.

For example, dominoes and marbles, toy car going down a ramp and hitting something, wooden planks sending a bouncy ball onto a seesaw.

- Pupils can then add the different elements together to create a chain covering the length set at the beginning.
- Make sure to record the different attempts so pupils can watch back and identify any problems before fixing them.

The results

The first object in the chain has potential energy. This could be because of its position, such as a ball at the top of a ramp, or its size, such as a book. When pushed or dropped, the kinetic energy of motion is transferred and aided by gravity knocking down or triggering the next object.

Extensions (try again but change something)

Option 1 – Specify how many obstacles or different materials need to be used; for example, pupils must have at least three different sections of the chain using three different materials, or pupils must include a ramp in the middle of their chain.

Adaptions

Option 1 – Set up a chain reaction that pupils can recreate with their materials.

Oobleck

Oobleck is a curious and strange phenomenon that creates a fun activity for everyone. It's a fun sensory activity as well as providing an opportunity to explore the science behind it, making it interesting for children of all ages.

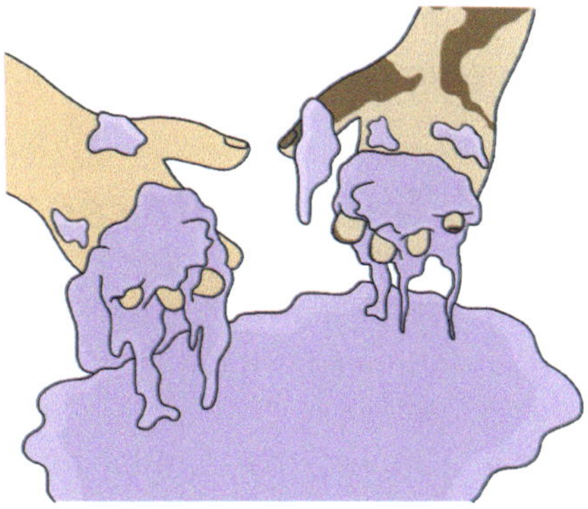

Question: How does applying pressure change the feeling of oobleck?

Hypothesis: The more pressure applied, the more solid the oobleck feels.

Items needed (quantities can be increased keeping the ratio between cornflour and water the same)

- Cornflour (75 g).
- Water (50 ml).
- Tray, jug, spoon.
- Food colouring (optional).

The experiment

- Mix the cornflour and water together in a jug.
- Add a couple of drops of your chosen food colouring and mix slowly.
- Pour the oobleck into the tray.
- Do not wash the oobleck down the drain, it will cause problems to the plumbing.

Lesson plan

- Allow your pupils to explore the oobleck; try scooping it with a spoon.
- Can they identify whether it is a solid or a liquid?
- Can they identify what is causing the oobleck to show characteristics of a solid *and* a liquid?

The results

Oobleck is a non-Newtonian fluid, as it has properties of both liquids and solids. If you put your hand slowly into the oobleck, it will react like a liquid; however if you apply pressure like squeezing or hitting it, the oobleck will react like a solid.

Extensions (try again but change something)

Option 1 – Supersize the experiment and add the oobleck to a large tray or small pool, and you can walk across it without sinking. It is recommended to wear wellies or be in bare feet.

Option 2 – Oobleck has similar features to quicksand, and so an experiment can be done to imitate this. Use a mixing bowl, a larger quantity of oobleck, and a plastic toy (it will need a higher surface area at the base). The toy can be "walked" across the oobleck with no problems; when the toy is released, it will begin to sink into the oobleck. Pupils can then try and pull the toy out. With pressure, the oobleck will become solid, making it difficult to remove.

Storm in a glass

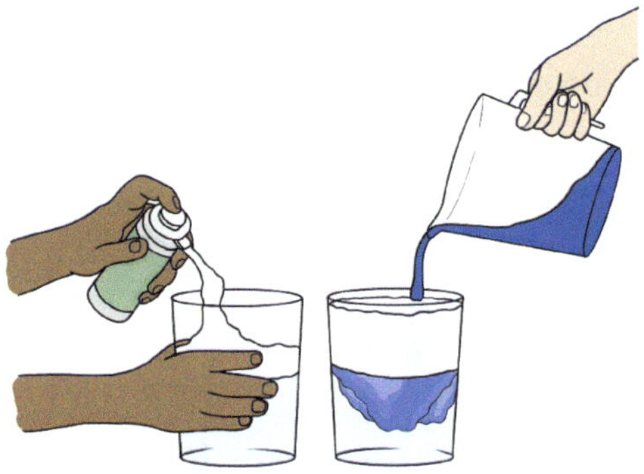

The storm in a glass is an interesting visualisation of rain. Clouds in the sky can hold millions of gallons of water, but at some point, they get too heavy, and the water falls out in the form of rain, sleet, snow, or hail.

Question: What happens to clouds when they become too full of water?

Hypothesis: Rainwater will fall from the clouds. The coloured water will fall from the shaving cream.

Items needed per group

- Water.
- Shaving cream.
- Blue food colouring.
- Two glasses.
- Spoon.

The experiment

- Fill the glass ½ full of water.
- Add shaving foam to the top of the water, and spread it out with your finger or a spoon. The top of the shaving foam needs to be flat. The glass should be about ¾ full.
- In the second glass, mix ½ a cup of water with ten drops of food colouring.
- Slowly add the coloured mix on top of the shaving cream using the spoon.
- As the shaving cream gets heavy with water, watch it seep out into the water below the shaving cream.

Lesson plan

- Show the pupils the experiment.
- Allow the pupils to recreate the storm on their own or working together.

The results

The storm in a glass uses the principles of density and precipitation. Density is the measurement of how compact a substance is within a certain space; in this experiment it is the density of the shaving cream that is important. When the clouds, or shaving cream, cannot hold any more water, it falls out or precipitates. We see this in the experiment when the water with the food colouring seeps out the bottom of the shaving cream.

Extensions (try again but change something)

Option 1 – Try changing the ratio of shaving cream and water, adding more water and less shaving cream or less water and more shaving cream. Which of them looks more like a drizzle and which more like a downpour?

Option 2 – Give the pupils different liquids to try the experiment with. Does it also work with orange juice or milk?

Dancing raisins

This activity is a fun way to explore densities with only a few ingredients. Watching the raisins dance opens the door to explaining more about how the experiment works. You can also explore densities by placing a ping pong ball or a rock in the glass.

Question: What will happen when the raisins are dropped in the vinegar and baking soda?

Hypothesis: The raisins will float up in the glass.

Items needed per group

- White vinegar (half glass/jug).
- Baking soda (1 tbsp).
- Raisins (cut into pieces).
- Water (half glass/jug).
- Clear glass or jug.
- Spoon.

The experiment

- Start with the glass/jug of water.
- Add the baking soda and stir it in until it is dissolved.
- Drop the cut raisins into the glass/jug.
- Pour in the vinegar; you may need to stir to get the dancing started.
- Watch as the raisins rise and fall in the glass/jug.

Lesson plan

- Split the class into small groups. The experiment is quite small, and this will allow them to see the experiment clearly.
- Each group will need a set of ingredients.
- For younger pupils, you can measure out the ingredients in advance. Older pupils can pour out the ingredients themselves.
- Raisins can be ripped by hand or cut with a knife.

The results

When the raisins are first dropped into the mixture, they sink to the bottom of the glass because they are denser than the liquid. The carbonated liquid releases carbon dioxide bubbles, which attach to the rough surface of the raisins. The bubbles act like tiny floatation devices, lifting the raisins to the top of the liquid due to the increase in buoyancy. When the bubbles reach surface, they pop, releasing the gas into the air. The raisin loses its buoyancy and sinks back to the bottom of the glass.

Extensions (try again but change something)

Option 1 – Set up three glasses and ask your pupils to change the ratios of baking soda and white vinegar to water. They can then compare the reaction of the raisins in each of the glasses.

Option 2 – Ask pupils to look at the raisins and think about what makes them good for the experiment. Can they think of any other ingredients that might work because they share similar features? For example, peanuts, lentils, or corn kernels.

Egg drop

The egg drop is a hands-on activity that requires pupils to think about the protective features of different materials and identify ways they can be connected together and used to shield the egg from the impact of a large fall.

Question: How can an egg be protected from breaking when falling?

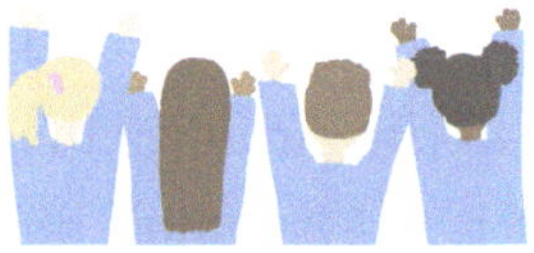

Hypothesis: The egg can be protected by insulating it and slowing the fall.

Items needed per group

- Eggs, one per group or pupil.
- Materials, e.g., cardboard, bubble wrap, tin foil, cling film, cloth, tissue paper.
- String, tape, glue.
- Upstairs window or other high place to drop eggs from.

The experiment

- Ask your pupils to protect the egg to prevent it from cracking or breaking when being dropped from your allocated location.
- Ask pupils what methods could be used to protect the egg.
- In their groups they may want to create a design of the protection.
- Supply all students with the materials; these could be allocated evenly between groups or provided to the whole class to choose from.
- Each individual/pair or group will need an egg. It is their job to protect the egg.
- When everyone is finished, or you have used the allotted time, take the eggs to the high location. Pupils should nominate one person from their group to drop the egg, everyone else can watch from the bottom.
- You may want to film the egg drops to watch back at a later point.
- When all of the eggs have been dropped, check each one for signs of cracking or breaking.
- Those whose eggs survived have successfully completed the challenge.

The results

Eggs are naturally very breakable, and a drop from an upstairs window is guaranteed to smash it. However, padding around the egg reduces the impact by absorbing some of the force, and an increased surface area like that of a parachute slows the fall, reducing the final impact.

Extensions (try again but change something)

Option 1 – Instead of providing a range of materials for pupils to choose freely from, give each material including the tape and glue a price. Provide each group with pretend money. The aim is to stay within budget and keep the egg safe. Pupils who keep the egg safe spending the least amount of money win.

Option 2 – Set a maximum weight for the pupils' creations. The aim is to stay under weight and keep the egg safe. Pupils who keep the egg safe with the lightest protection win.

Adaptions

Option 1 – Provide pupils with plans of how to build an egg protector and parachute with a list of the materials and instructions on how to build it. By following the instructions accurately, pupils should keep their egg safe.

Bottle xylophone

This experiment allows pupils to experiment with pitch (frequency of the sound) and timbre (quality of sound) with a simple instrument that they can adapt. They are able to create their own instrument before playing it and making changes to experiment with the sounds it makes.

Question: How does changing the amount of water in a glass change the sound it makes when hit?

Hypothesis: The more water in the glass the lower the sound will be.

Items needed per group

- Glass bottles or glasses of the same size.
- Water.
- Pencil.
- Cling film/plastic wrap.
- Food colouring.
- Paper and coloured pens.

The experiment

- Line up the bottles.
- Pour a different amount of water into each bottle. Starting at one end, each bottle should have increasing amounts of water.
- Cover the top of the bottles with cling film to preserve the amount of water.
- Using a pencil, hit each of the bottles one by one and listen to the sounds made.

Lesson plan 1 – Small groups/pairs

- Add a couple of drops of food colouring to each bottle so that each bottle has a different colour.
- Line up the bottles in order of increasing amounts of water.
- Using a pencil to hit the bottles, the pupils can experiment making music.

- By identifying the colours that they are using, pupils can write down their music. Draw coloured dots to represent each of bottles. They may want to write a line for each person in the group and play at the same time.
- Once they have their music written down, try moving the pupils to another group's xylophone and following their music.

The results

This bottle xylophone is made up of a series of wind instruments, each tuned to a specific note depending on the amount of air in the bottle or glass. When the pencil hits the glass, the bottle vibrates creating air waves. The larger the air tunnel, as in a bottle with only a little water, the higher the note that we hear.

Extensions (try again but change something)

Option 1 – Using a tuner app on a phone or tablet, pupils can match the notes of their bottles to musical notes. They will need to carefully add or remove water until the tuner hits the intended note. By creating an octave of notes using seven bottles, they will be able to play simple songs using their pencil and xylophone.

Option 2 – Try changing one of the parts of the experiment. What happens if you use something else as the drumstick? How does it sound different if you use a thick or thin glass? Does the sound change if you use something other than water in the bottles?

Bridge building

Building a bridge is a seemingly simple task; however, to ensure it can hold weight, it needs to be built using specific shapes. The same technique is used in building roofs. This activity combines the physics of building a bridge with teamwork and communication.

Question: What bridge building formation will best hold the weight of a toy car?

Hypothesis: The bridge will hold under heavier weights if made from a series of triangles.

Items needed per group

- Marshmallows.
- Raw spaghetti.
- Toy car.

The experiment

- Pupils can complete this activity individually, in pairs, or in groups.
- Start by providing a gap to build the bridges over. This could be a gap between two tables or two piles of books.
- Each group should take some marshmallows and spaghetti to a workspace.
- To create a structure, insert the pieces of spaghetti into the marshmallows. The marshmallows will act as the glue between the spaghetti strands.
- Encourage pupils to experiment with shapes and lengths of spaghetti.
- They should ensure that their bridge covers the full width of the gap.
- Once complete, they should put the bridge over the gap and test whether it can bear the weight of a toy car.
- If the bridge does not withstand the test, encourage the pupils to try again but using a different technique.

The results

When force is applied to one of the corners of a triangle, the pressure is distributed down the sides, squeezing the triangle. Bridges are often built using multiple triangles. Compression happens on the outer sides of the triangles, and tension happens on the inner and bottom sides of the triangles. Different types of triangles can be used in different formations.

Extensions (try again but change something)

Option 1 – Give pupils a specific number of marshmallows and pieces of spaghetti to use. They will need to think more carefully about how they build the bridge. They may also need to plan the bridge before they start building.

Option 2 – Pupils will need access to the internet to search for a famous bridge or a local bridge. The challenge is to try and build the bridge as a replica of the real one. Can they identify the features of the bridge that keep it up and that mean it can support heavy weights?

Adaptions

Option 1 – Provide pupils with a simple plan of how to build the bridge that they can copy using the marshmallows and spaghetti.

Balloon cars

Newton's laws of motion can be difficult to comprehend; however, this activity includes them in an interesting experiment that requires pupils to build a car. Watching the movement of the car will support explaining the laws.

Question: What happens to the car when air from the balloon is pushed out the back?

Hypothesis: The car will move forward when air is expelled out the back.

Items needed per group

- Plastic bottle/small cardboard box.
- Bottle caps (four of the same for each car)/circles cut out of cardboard.
- Balloon.
- Wooden skewers (two per car).
- Straws (three per car).
- Tape.
- Scissors.
- Craft knife.
- Rubber band.

The experiment

- The bottle will be the body of the car. Cut two straws so they are longer than the width of the bottle.
- Tape them to the bottom of the bottle (across the width), making sure they are parallel.
- Cut the skewers slightly longer than the straws.
- Cut a small hole in the centre of each bottle lid.
- Thread one bottle lid onto the pointed end of the skewer and push to the opposite end. Thread the skewer through the straw and then add a second bottle lid. Repeat to create the second axel and wheels.
- Check the car rolls forward and backwards to test the axels move smoothly.

- Slide the third straw into the balloon and tie it on with the elastic band. Blow up the balloon through the straw, checking for leaks.
- Cut a hole in the top of the bottle, big enough for the straw, and thread the straw through and out the mouth of the bottle. Tape the straw to the mouth of the bottle ensuring it points backwards.
- Inflate the balloon, then cover the end of the straw with your finger as you put it on the floor.
- When you are ready to race, let go of the straw and let the car go.

Lesson plan

- The pupils can work together or alone to build a car. Encourage them to design their car to be the most efficient.
- When they are finished building, set up a racecourse with a start and finish line, and test which car finishes and how fast they finish.

The results

Newton's third law of motion states that for every action, there will be an equal and opposite reaction – as the balloon deflates, the escaping air is pushed out of the back of the car and the car moves forward. Newton's second law of motion states that the net force acting on an object equals its mass times its acceleration, seen as the car accelerates when the balloon deflates and decelerates to a stop when friction slows it down. The car continuing to move forwards until stopped by an outside force, friction, is Newton's first law of motion.

Extensions (try again but change something)

Option 1 – Ask the pupils to think of ways to make the cars run further or move faster. This might include blowing up the balloon more, reducing the weight of the car, reducing the car's air resistance, or holding a piece of cardboard behind the car for the air to push off.

Reference list

1. Westwell, M. and Panizzon, D., 2018. Becoming explorers of our world: The purpose of science education. In R. Gregson (Ed.), *Connecting with science education* (pp.22–40). South Melbourne, Victoria, Australia: Oxford University Press.

2. Kalogiannakis, M., Papadakis, S. and Zourmpakis, A.I., 2021. Gamification in science education. A systematic review of the literature. *Education Sciences, 11*(1), p.22.

3. National Curriculum in England: Science Programmes of Study. https://www.gov.uk/government/publications/national-curriculum-in-england-science-programmes-of-study/national-curriculum-in-england-science-programmes-of-study

Chapter 7
OUTDOOR LEARNING

In today's rapidly evolving educational landscape, where the digital world often takes precedence, connecting with the natural environment has never been more important. The chapter on outdoor learning looks into the critical need for integrating nature into children's educational experiences and the benefits of outdoor learning, extending from advancing gross motor skills to improved self-regulation. This chapter uncovers the myriad benefits of the natural world to human well-being and child development.

The inclusion of practical activities, such as scavenger hunts and natural art, serves as a bridge that links theoretical insights with hands-on experiences. These activities are designed not only to foster an appreciation and understanding of the environment but also to cultivate observation skills, creativity, and a sense of belonging in the world around us. Many of the lesson plans include adaptations to ensure that outdoor learning is accessible and extensions to engage and enrich every child.

Going outside has extensive benefits for children, including cognitive and socio-emotional benefits for outdoor learning, including the use of human-made outdoor settings [1]. Outdoor learning is believed to be a low-cost, non-invasive pedagogical solution to public health challenges such as mental health and improving physical activity. Research has shown that travelling to a forest or outdoor centre is not essential, and forest schools are one aspect of outdoor learning, especially in schools with limited access to outdoor spaces [2]. While some of the activities in this chapter require specific items, it is possible to complete most of them in a playground and easy to collect items such as leaves and sticks.

Another key aspect of outdoor learning is the development of children's gross motor skills. Schools often focus on cognitive development, with the pressure of test scores and academic curriculum; however, the development of motor skills is an inseparable part of children's lives [3]. The natural environment acts as a dynamic classroom, presenting limitless opportunities for exploration and curiosity-driven learning. Beyond its contribution to gross motor skill development, outdoor learning offers multifaceted benefits that encompass emotional, social, and environmental understanding. Children enhance their

DOI: 10.4324/9781003515234-8

physical abilities by engaging in activities such as climbing, jumping, and running, and learning valuable lessons in resilience, teamwork, and self-awareness.

Spending time outdoors has many benefits for children's mental health and self-regulation, as it promotes constructive imaginative, collaborative play, and self-confidence by increasing the likelihood of taking risks and seeking adventure [4]. These positive effects of nature on children's well-being underscore the significance of integrating outdoor activities into their daily routines. Exposure to natural settings can also foster a sense of environmental stewardship, encouraging children to appreciate and protect the natural world as they grow. Simply spending time in green spaces, including parks, play areas, and gardens, has been shown to reduce stress and mental fatigue, with links being made to the reduction of behaviours stemming from ADHD [5]. Simply being in view of nature, there is an improved level of interest and attention, and decreased feelings of fear and anger [6].

The sensory experiences provided by the natural world can stimulate cognitive development and creativity, further illustrating the multifaceted benefits of outdoor time for children. Emphasising the importance of these natural interactions, educators and parents can play a pivotal role in ensuring children reap the extensive mental, emotional, and physical benefits of spending time in nature.

By the end of this chapter, the reader is left with a deeper recognition of the outdoors as a dynamic classroom that is vast, vibrant, and vitally important to our collective future. This exploration into outdoor learning is an essential read for anyone committed to nurturing well-rounded, environmentally conscious individuals equipped to face tomorrow's challenges with resilience, curiosity, and a deep-rooted connection to the natural world.

Note

Some activities in this chapter involve the use of sharp tools, such as craft knives or potato peelers. To ensure the safety of all involved, these activities should be closely supervised by an adult at all times. When completing the activities with younger pupils, you could run two activities simultaneously: A small group works with one adult to complete the actions involving the sharp tool, and the remainder of the class works on something different.

Activities included in this chapter

Activity	Whole class	Groups	Pairs	Individuals	Extensions	Adaptions
Scavenger hunt						
Natural art						
Minibeast hotel						
Dam building						
Woodland Olympics						
Giant sundial						
Leaf boats						
Musical nature						
Wood whittling						
Design a greenspace						

Scavenger hunt

Getting outside and exploring is a great way to learn more about the world around you and encourages children to look in more detail at their surroundings. This activity gives them a reason to get outside and some direction in what to do when they get outside.

Aims

To use their observation skills to engage with the environment around them.

Items needed per group

- Pen/pencil (1).
- Paper (1).
- Card (2).
- Felt tip pens (2).
- Hole punch/craft knife (2).

Lesson plan 1 – Small groups/pairs

- Each pupil will need to start with a piece of paper and pen. They will be creating a scavenger hunt for their peers.
- Down the left side of the page, draw small boxes.
- Next to each box, pupils should write an item to find outside. This could include specific items or descriptions of items.
- Pupils could also add drawings of the items to find.
- Pupils should then swap their scavenger hunts.
- Head outside, and each child should look for the items included on the list they have been given.
- You could give the pupils a specific number of items to add to the list and then a time limit to find the items.

Examples of scavenger hunt items include round leaf, spiky leaf, stick smaller than your hand, leaf bigger than your hand, flower, woodlouse, ladybird, something of a specific colour or shape, or something soft.

Lesson plan 2 – Individuals

- Each child will need a piece of card. Using a felt tip pen, they should draw the face of a lion, horse, or another animal with lots of hair. You could provide them with an image to copy.
- Once the drawing is complete, they should cut it out.
- Using the hole punch or craft knife with adult supervision, each pupil should add holes to the hair section of their animal.
- Taking their card animals outside, look around for flowers and leaves and poke them through the holes to fill in the hair of the animal.
- Once finished, make sure to take a photo of the piece before the flowers wilt.

Adaptions

Option 1 (lesson plan 1) – Provide the pupils with a pre-made worksheet of items to find rather than asking them to create their own.

Natural art

This activity requires children to use their basic knowledge of art to create images using materials they can find outside. Art involving nature is a simple way to display the beauty of the natural world and to create a tactile piece at the same time. This activity definitely works best when there is no wind so that the materials don't blow away!

Aims

To create a piece of art using natural materials.

Items needed per group

- Sticks.
- Natural materials.
- Chalk (2).

Lesson plan 1 – Individuals

- Each child will need to start by creating a frame with four sticks. This works well on mown grass or paving.
- They will then need to collect natural materials. These could include leaves, sticks, stones, feathers, flowers, or sand.
- Using the materials they have collected, each child should create a portrait of themselves or one of their classmates.
- Encourage them to think about the shape of the face, including all of the facial features and the texture of their hair.
- When they're finished, make sure to take a photo. Alternatively, give each child a piece of card and some PVA glue, so they can then stick the materials onto the card, creating a semi-permanent version of their portrait.

Lesson plan 2 – Whole class/small groups

- As a class or group, choose an image that can be drawn out in the playground or on a giant piece of paper.
- Using the chalk, draw the outline of the image on the playground.

- The pupils will then need to collect lots of materials they can use to fill in the image. They should think of collecting things of different colours and shades of the same colour, for example, a variety leaves in different shades of green.
- They may want to use sticks or stones to follow the outline before filling in the image with other materials.
- Once finished, make sure to take a photo of the artwork.

Extensions

Option 1 (lesson plan 1) – Pupils could create a full-body portrait using a variety of materials to highlight the difference between the skin and the clothes.

Option 2 – This works for both lesson plans. Talk about how different shapes show highlights and shadows in different places. Can the pupils find a way to incorporate this into their natural art using only natural objects?

Adaptions

Option 1 (lesson plan 1) – Give each pupil a piece of chalk to plan out their image before they start adding the materials. Alternatively, give each child a printout of a simple face that they can cover with natural materials.

Minibeast hotel

Building a minibeast hotel in your greenspace helps to attract beneficial insects by providing a safe space for them to hide away and also uses your garden waste. A minibeast hotel can attract anything from ladybirds and woodlice to hedgehogs and toads.

Aims

To create a safe space for the bugs in your green space.

Items needed per group

- Wooden pallet or planks of wood and bricks (1).
- Bricks, toilet roll tubes, strips of cardboard, bamboo canes, broken plant pots, cleaned-out plastic bottles with the bottom cut off, empty tin cans

Lesson plan 1 – Whole class

- Head outside and look for bugs. Note where you find them and the environment around them. Is it sunny or shaded? Is it wet or dry? Are there lots of leaves?
- Pupils could work together or on their own to collect materials such as leaves, sticks, bark, grass, pinecones, stones, or leaf litter.
- You could also provide bricks, toilet roll tubes, strips of cardboard, bamboo canes, broken plant pots, cleaned-out plastic bottles with the bottom cut off, or empty tin cans.
- Clear a space near bushes and trees, so the bugs can easily find it. You will need a flat base for the best building space.
- Start by creating a frame to build the minibeast hotel. A wooden pallet works well, or you can build a frame using bricks and wooden planks.
- The pupils can then fill the different sections with the materials they have collected. Encourage them to use a variety of materials that they have found and think the bugs might enjoy.

Lesson plan 2 – Small groups/pairs/individuals

- Head outside and look for bugs. Note where you find them and the environment around them. Is it sunny or shaded? Is it wet or dry? Are there lots of leaves?
- Pupils could work together or on their own to collect materials such as leaves, sticks, bark, grass, pinecones, stones, or leaf litter.
- You could also provide bricks, toilet roll tubes, strips of cardboard, bamboo canes, broken plant pots, cleaned-out plastic bottles with the bottom cut off, or empty tin cans.
- Each group/pair/individual will need to find a space near a hedge or some trees.
- They can then start to build their minibeast hotel. Encourage them to create a frame and include at least two different materials.

Extensions

Option 1 – Pupils should have a look in books or online to see where bigger animals such as hedgehogs and toads like to live and what they could do to ensure their minibeast hotel is able to house them alongside the bugs. What do they need to include for the larger animals to feel safe too?

Adaptions

Option 1 – Provide the pupils with a cardboard box with the top cut off. Encourage them to fill the box with a variety of materials before placing it outside for the bugs to explore.

Dam building

This activity is a good way of team building while working on the problem solving of stopping water from continuing down a stream. Out in the world, beavers effect their environment by using natural materials to block the flow of water to create a deep pool where they can make their home safe from predators.

Due to needing to block all the water from the stream, if there is only one water source available, this activity would work well in rotation with other small group activities. When pupils are finished, make sure to return the environment to the way you found it.

Aims

To work as a team to block a stream of water by making a dam.

Items needed per group

- Waterproof clothing.
- Mud, sticks, stones.
- Stream.

To create your own stream, dig a channel or create two rows of stones and cover with a waterproof liner. Place gravel along the bottom of the liner. Use a hose to send water down from one end of the stream or pour water from a bucket into the stream to test the dam.

Lesson plan 1 – Small groups

- The first thing to do is find an area of the stream that can be reached to block off with a dam.
- Collect a variety of sticks and stones that can be used.
- Working as a team, the children should try to use the sticks and stones to block the water. Ask them to think about how to fill any gaps with smaller materials.
- Their dam will need to stay standing despite water building up behind it adding pressure to the dam.

- Talk about how beavers use this deep pool of water to stay safe from predators and store fresh branches as a food source in the winter.
- Talk about the effects of the dam on the rest of the stream of water.

Extensions

Option 1 – Using the materials that they have collected, instead of building a dam to stop the water, encourage the children to try and divert the water to follow a different course. An example of this in the real world is the creation of meanders in rivers around obstacles or the straightening of rivers as they wear away at the ground or the corner.

Adaptions

Option 1 – Set up a plastic tray and build a wall in the middle of the tray. When finished, add water to one side of the tray and look for gaps in the wall that you built. Fix any gaps with extra materials such as mud or small stones.

Woodland Olympics

Working as a team or independently to complete this challenge tests balance, coordination, strength, and speed, as well as communication and confidence. Each activity requires pupils to focus on different skills, and they all require an awareness of the forest space you are playing in.

Aims

To take part in an outdoor sports event and develop fundamental movement skills.

Items needed per group

- Forest or woodland space.
- Stopwatch.
- String.
- Paper, pen, and clipboard for results.

Lesson plan 1 – Whole class

- Split the class into four teams; each team should choose a team name. Write the names at the top of the piece of paper, and the names of each of the competitions down the left-hand side.
- Pupils can nominate a person for each competition, or everyone can compete.
- Using leaves of different sizes and colours, pupils can make medals for the winners. Make a small hole in the leaf or tie the string to the stem of the leaf to make the medal.

Natural obstacle course – Using the environment around you, set up a course. It could be using what is already available or moving items that pupils find. Examples could include a tree slalom, crawling under low branches, jumping over stones, making a ladder out of sticks to hop through, balancing across a fallen tree, spinning in circles through flowers, or frog-jumping through puddles.

Twig relay – Set up a starting point and a course for the pupils to run. This could be a longer course with points for the changeover to take place or two points for pupils to run to and back from before handing over the stick to the next person. Each team will need a stick to use for the relay baton.

Pinecone shot put – Gather some pinecones and set a start line. Each pupil will need to stand on the start line and throw their pinecone. The pupil who throws their pinecone the furthest wins. This could be measured in heats, a member of each team throwing a pinecone and being placed. They then earn points depending on their place within the heat.

Act like an animal – Line the children up with a start and finish line or a space to move around in. Their challenge is to act like the animal you shout out. Points can be earned for style or realism. Examples could include wiggle like a worm, prowl like a lion, buzz like a honeybee, soar like an owl, scuttle like a mouse, stomp like a bear, nibble like a squirrel, peck like a woodpecker, or chomp like a crocodile.

Long jump – Create a giant leaf pile to jump into or clear a space to jump into; choose a large stick where the children have to stand before jumping. Measure the distance jumped using footsteps, or mark the distances jumped in the ground along the side of the space being used for jumping.

Tree balance beam – Fallen trees make great balance beams. The challenge is to see how far across each pupil can get without touching the floor or using someone else to support. Can anyone get across by hopping? Or with their hands behind their back?

Adaptions

Option 1 – For students with limited mobility or those using mobility aids, you can bring natural items to the playground and draw out some obstacles using chalk.

Giant sundial

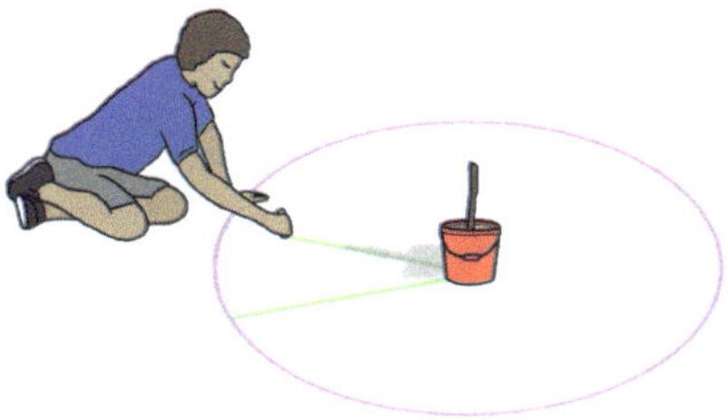

The sun's light makes objects cast shadows across the ground. This has long been used as a method of telling the time. The earliest known sundial was made by the Egyptians in about 3500 BC and was as simple as a stick in the ground that cast a shadow. As the sun moves through the sky, the direction of the shadow changes, giving an indication of how far through the day it is.

Aims

To create a giant sundial which can be used to tell the time.

Items needed per group

- Sunny day.
- Chalk/pebbles (1).
- String (1).
- Bucket of sand/soil (1).
- Large stick (1).
- Paper plate (2).
- Pencil (2).
- Straw (2).

Lesson plan 1 – Whole class/small groups

- One pupil will need to hold the piece of string in one spot; another will take the other end of the string and pull it tight. Using the chalk, they will draw a big circle using the string as a compass. If you are completing the activity on grass, a second piece of string could be used to create the circle, then hold it down with stones.
- In the centre of the circle, place the bucket of sand or soil, and put the stick in facing straight up.
- Using the chalk or pebbles, mark out the location of the shadow and write down the time.
- Return every hour and mark out a line for each time.

Lesson plan 2 – Individuals

- Each pupil will need a paper plate and a straw.
- Punch a hole in the middle of the plate using a pencil and put the straw through, securing it in an upright position.
- Take the sundial outside and place it in a flat sunny area. The sundial will need to be kept in the same place all day.
- Each hour, on the hour, draw a line following the shadow. Write the time at the end of the line.
- By the end of the school day, you will have a partially completed sundial.
- Pupils could take them home and complete in the evening and the following morning using the lines they've already added as reference for setting it up.
- The following day, remove the clock from your classroom and ask pupils to put away their watches. Try and use the sundials to tell the time through the day. They may need to add additional lines to show quarter past, half past, and quarter to the hour to be more accurate.

Adaptions

Option 1 (lesson plan 2) – Provide pupils with a printed image of a sundial that can be cut out and stuck to the top of the paper plate. They can then add a straw and they will be able to use the sundial straight away.

Leaf boats

Leaf boats are simple structures carefully put together using a variety of natural materials. They can be as simple or as complex as you like, adding sails and decorations to make them look impressive. But be careful it doesn't become too heavy for the hull and start to sink!

Aims

To create a boat that can float and move using natural objects.

Items needed per group

- Pond/tray of water.
- Bark/tie together a few twigs to make the hull.
- Leaves.
- Twig.
- Mud.
- Flowers.

Lesson plan 1 – Pairs/individuals

- Head outside to collect your materials.
- Each pair/individual will need to start with a piece of bark to make the base (or hull) of the boat. Place the bark rough side down.
- Collect some mud or mix some soil with a small amount of water and put it in the centre of the bark.
- Place the twig upright in the mud to create the mast.
- Thread one or two leaves onto the twig to create the sails.
- Add some small flowers onto the boat for decoration.
- Place the leaf boat onto the water and let it set sail.
- Set a start and finish line, then let the boats float across the water to see which makes it there first.

- Encourage pupils to think about how their boats might move faster, for example if they were to blow into the leaves like the wind.

Extensions

Option 1 – Pupils can try making leaf boats with multiple masts to increase the speed of their leaf boat. Ask pupils to look at images of large sailing boats and replicate their sail structure.

Option 2 – Test out how much weight the leaf boats can handle before they stop moving and start to sink. This could be done using Lego minifigures as sailors or small pebbles as weights.

Adaptions

Option 1 – A simplified leaf boat can be made using two leaves. Start with one as the base; this is the hull of the boat. Use the stem of the second leaf to poke a hole in the centre of the first. The second leaf should then stand upright in the middle of the first leaf forming the sail of the boat.

Musical nature

There are lots of sounds that can be found in nature, from the rustle of leaves to the chirping of birds. Many people feel calmed by the sounds found in nature; listening to the ocean or the sound of rain helps many people fall asleep. This activity gives children time to consider the sounds found in nature and how they can recreate them.

Aims

To explore the sounds that can be found in nature and replicate them using natural materials.

Items needed per group

- Something to record with such as a phone or tablet.
- Paper.
- Clipboard.
- Pen/paper.

Lesson plan 1 – Whole class/small groups

- Take a walk outside, preferably to a quiet area with little man-made noise, and find somewhere to sit down. Ask the children to stay quiet and listen to the world around them.
- Let them try and identify the different sounds and what is making them.
- Their next task is to try and find items around them that can be used to recreate the sounds.
- They could find sticks or stones to hit or rub together, leaves to shake, make a xylophone from sticks, or use seeds or soil to turn into a shaker.
- Once they have collected items to create an instrument, head inside.
- Give each child a chance to try out making sounds with the items they brought inside.
- Once the children have had time to make sounds on their own, take some time to talk about different outside locations.
- For example, if they were in the rainforest, what sounds might they hear? Can they use shakers to make the sound of rain, or the shaking of leaves for the wind?

- One of the pupils could become the conductor of the orchestra and use their hand gestures to control the volume of different instruments.
- Try recording the sounds that the class makes and then listen back to it.

Lesson plan 2 – Pairs/individuals

- Head outside for a walk, preferably to a quiet area with little man-made noise and find somewhere to sit down. Ask the children to stay quiet and listen to the world around them.
- Let them try and identify the different sounds and what is making them.
- After spending some time walking around in silence, each child/pair will need a piece of paper and clipboard or whiteboard to lean on.
- Each child/pair will need to draw a map of the area.
- They will need to walk around the area again and find some specific sounds that they can hear. Looking at their map, they should mark them on the map.
- Once they have finished their maps and added on some sounds, they should swap maps with their peers.
- Following one of their peers maps, they should try and find the sounds marked on the map.

Extensions

Option 1 – Older pupils could use a craft knife to cut notches in a stick to make a rasp. Or tie a piece of string to a curved piece of wood, which makes a twang sound when pulled and let go.

Wood whittling

Sticks are often used as part of imaginative play. Whittling them gives them a more specific purpose from wands and marshmallow sticks to spoons and animals. Wood whittling or carving is a creative way to introduce knife skills to children; it requires the use of their fine motor skills and lots of concentration. It is also highly rewarding, as each movement of the peeler changes the shape of the stick.

Due to the use of sharp tools, this activity is safest with a high ratio of adults to children, especially with younger pupils.

Aims

To obtain basic knowledge of how to whittle a stick and be confident in using the appropriate tools safely.

Items needed per group

- Strong stick (young, fresh wood that has not dried out is best; recommended tree types include silver birch, willow, sycamore, alder, and lime).
- Potato peeler (a straight peeler works best).
- Sandpaper.

Lesson plan – Individuals

- Before starting the whittling, go over the safety of using sharp tools with the pupils. Always whittle away from yourself towards the ground, hold the handle not the blade, stay seated while using the peeler, and point the peeler at the ground when walking with it.
- Find somewhere comfortable to sit.
- Each pupil will need a strong stick and a peeler to start with.
- Holding the stick with one hand, place the end of the stick on the ground.
- The first task is to remove all of the bark from the stick. Use the blade of the peeler to carefully scrape the bark away. Always peel towards the ground.

- When they have removed all of the bark, the pupils can start to shape the stick.
- They might want to make thinner sections or add notches into the wood. Whittling works best when small amounts of wood are removed each time.
- Each pupil will then need a piece of sandpaper. By rubbing the sandpaper on the stick they can make it smooth.
- Using the pointed end of the peeler, the pupils can carve patterns or messages into the smooth sides of the stick. They could also add their initials or name so they know whose is whose.
- The sticks could also be decorated with leaves, string, feathers, flowers, or paint to make a magic wand.

Extensions

Option 1 – Whittle a simple flower. Start by removing the bark from a straight twig. Instead of removing pieces of the stick, peel back thin strips from the tip of the stick and open them out to create the petals. Further down the stick, add a couple of additional peeled back strips to form the leaves.

Adaptions

Option 1 – Ask pupils to remove the bark from their sticks using the peeler. They can then use the sandpaper to smooth it out and skip straight to decorating with leaves, string, feathers, flowers, or paint.

Design a greenspace

The environment around us is important, from the air we breath to the plants and animals we share our world with. We must conserve our environment so that it can continue to provide for us; this includes water, nutrients, energy, raw materials, and food. Over time, humans have changed the environment to try and make life better but in turn have created other problems such as air pollution, biodiversity loss, and plastic waste. This activity asks pupils to try and create a space that humans can share with the plants and animals around them.

Aims

To design a greenspace for humans to enjoy. To consider how plants and animals can be included in a greenspace.

Items needed per group

- Paper.
- Coloured pens/pencils/crayons.
- Access to the internet.

Lesson plan 1 – Whole class/ small groups/pairs/individuals

- This activity can be done alone or with pupils working together to make one piece.
- Take a walk to a local green space and note down the important features. What makes it a green space? What do people like about it? Are there lots of trees? What are the paths made of?
- Find or take some pictures of the place at the moment and talk about whether it creates pollution, whether there is anywhere for bugs or animals to live, whether there are trees creating shaded space, whether there is natural sunlight, etc.
- The children should try to think of how they could make an area into their ideal greenspace; this could be starting from scratch or adapting what is already available.

- Start by drawing a map of the area, including anything that is permanent such as buildings or roads.
- Once this is done, think of what could be added to make the space more green.

Examples might include flower or vegetable beds, tree-covered picnic area, moss or green roofs, grass area, woodland hideouts for bugs, stepping stone paths, or natural material playground.

Extensions

Option 1 – Use graph/squared paper for this activity. Give students a specific area and encourage them to find out the size of the items they want to add to the space. They should think about how much space wheelchair users or prams need to pass by stationary objects and how the shade of a large tree might effect the growth of a flower bed.

Option 2 – Make a list of specific items including trees, path materials, playground equipment, etc. and their prices (these do not have to be realistic and can be adapted to the maths level of the pupils). Give the pupils a budget for their space and ask them to design their space within budget.

Adaptions

Option 1 – Provide cut out images of different items that pupils might want to include in their greenspace. Using a glue stick, they can put together their perfect green space using the materials provided.

Reference List

1. Mann, J., Gray, T., Truong, S., Sahlberg, P., Bentsen, P., Passy, R., Ho, S., Ward, K. and Cowper, R., 2021. A systematic review protocol to identify the key benefits and efficacy of nature-based learning in outdoor educational settings. *International Journal of Environmental Research and Public Health, 18*(3), p.1199.

2. Williams, R. and Scott, C., 2019. The current state of outdoor learning in a UK secondary setting: Exploring the benefits, drawbacks and recommendations. *ABC Journal of Advanced Research, 8*(2), pp.109–122.

3. Arifianti, E. and Agustiningsih, R., 2024. Development of an outdoor play-based learning model to train gross motor skills in early childhood. *Kinestetik: Jurnal Ilmiah Pendidikan Jasmani, 8*(2), pp.275–281.

4. Sustainable Development Commission, 2010. Every child's future matters. St Andrews Research Repository, University of St Andrews.

5. Taylor, A., et al. 2001. Coping with ADD: The surprising connection to green play settings. *Environment and Behavior, 33*, pp.54–77.

6. Burdette, H. and Whitaker, R. 2005. Resurrecting free play in young children: Looking beyond fitness and to attention, affiliation, and affect. *Archives of Pediatrics & Adolescent Medicine, 159*(1), pp.46–50.

Chapter 8
ART

Art is a vibrant and universal language that speaks to us across time and space. Art offers children the opportunity to explore, understand, and express themselves in unique and creative ways. This chapter will dive into the world of art education with clear links to the primary curriculum. Each activity focusses on a variety of techniques and materials while looking deeper into the work of specific artists. Art has a constant presence in our communities and workplaces, from graffiti to art galleries, each piece giving insight into the artist and their message.

The earliest known examples of art on a flat surface date back over 30,000 years, featuring naturalistic animal figures and stylised or partial images of humans [1]. Some pieces featured engravings in stone; others used pigments to create colour or finger drawings on soft surfaces. Through the years, art has developed using a large breadth of materials and techniques to convey emotions and meaning. The activities aim to light the spark of creativity in young minds through engaging activities and thoughtful discussion. By introducing students to the works of great artists and guiding them in the exploration of their own creative processes, we not only cultivate their artistic skills but also enrich their personal and social development.

The arts did not become a part of the national curriculum until 1988. Since then, the presence of arts within primary schools has seen a considerable increase, reflecting a broader understanding of its value in fostering creativity, emotional expression, and cognitive development among young learners [2]. Despite the clear benefits associated with engaging students in artistic endeavours, the reality within the educational context often presents a challenge. Traditional academic disciplines' rigorous demands and priorities leave minimal room for arts education, relegating it to the sidelines. This limitation confines the opportunities for artistic exploration and restricts the potential developmental benefits it can offer. The activities in this chapter aim to provide teachers with a variety of different activities that can be used as whole-class art lessons or time fillers for wet-weather play times. By offering these activities, the hope is to bridge the gap between the rich potential of arts education and the practical challenges of curriculum time pressures. In doing so, it

DOI: 10.4324/9781003515234-9

underlines the importance of creativity and artistic expression as fundamental components of a well-rounded education.

Research shows significant positives in art education, from the development of complex thought processes and improved creative thinking to stimulating curiosity and emotional resilience [3]. Art also shows great benefits in therapeutic interventions, showing progress in the ability to pay attention and focus, emotional regulation, and confidence [4]. Art gives pupils a form to express themselves. It is accessible to pupils at all levels and has been proven to benefit pupils in both mainstream and special education. It has also been crucial in allowing access to other areas of the curriculum traditionally taught through written and spoken language [5].

Not only can artwork be completed as an individual activity, but art can also be a collaborative exercise supporting communication and teamwork. While the activities in this chapter are written with individual pupils in mind, each can be turned into a group project with a bigger canvas! This is a great opportunity for classroom decoration or completing a community project. If you choose to create group projects, make sure to take photos of the art so each pupil has something that can be added to their sketchbook or taken home to show family.

Finally, the chapter features a variety of artists, some of whom are famous and recognised in many classrooms as important figures in the art world, and others are less known in education. It is important to recognise that despite the high proportion of female artists throughout history, few were represented in museums and galleries until more recently [6]. This can still be seen in the artists that are regarded as important to teach in schools. The inclusion of lesser-known artists in this chapter is an attempt to redress the balance.

Progress in line with the National Curriculum [7]

KS1 – *Learn to use a range of materials creatively and use drawing, painting and sculpture to develop and share ideas. Develop a wide range of art and design techniques by using colour, pattern, texture, line, shape, form and space. Learn about the work of a range of artists, craft makers, and designers, identifying similarities and differences between each other and their own work.*

KS2 – *Develop techniques, including their control and use of materials with creativity and experimentation. Create sketchbooks and record observations that can be reviewed and revisited. Improve art and design techniques, including drawing, painting and sculpture, with a variety of materials. Learn about great artists, architects and designers in history.*

The chapter includes activities that explore a variety of materials and techniques for creating art. Each activity highlights a key skill, such as colour mixing, or explores the work of a specific artist, such as Wassily Kandinsky. The artwork created by pupils can spark discussion around the techniques and materials used and how their work compares to the artists they are studying.

Activities included in this chapter

Activity	Whole class	Groups	Pairs	Individuals	Extensions	Adaptions
Messy paint						
Bubble painting						
Potato printing						
Wax designs						
Tea staining						
String painting						
African silhouettes						
Tissue paper window						
Skittles patterns						
Polka dot painting						

Messy paint

One of the best parts about art is that it is completely up to interpretation. Often we encourage children to draw something that they know, like a house, a flower, or a mountain, but there is also space within art to draw things like music or emotion.

Aims

To create a piece of art based on how you feel.

Artist: *Wassily Kandinsky*

Kandinsky had a rare condition called synaesthesia, which meant he would see colours when he heard music and hear music when painting. Kandinsky theorised that colour directly affects the emotions of people. Instead of painting realistically, he used colour to show emotions.

Items needed per group

- Paint.
- Paper (each pupil will need a piece of paper for each type of music).
- Blocks, cars, brushes, sponges, string. etc.
- Music (variety of types e.g., rock, classical, pop).

Lesson plan 1 – Whole class

- Give each child their own piece of paper. Ask them to write the number 1 on the back of the first piece.
- All pupils should have access to a variety of paint colours and tools that they can use with the paint.
- Start playing the first piece of music. Encourage the pupils to paint and draw in a way that they feel fits with the music.
- After a few minutes, stop the music and ask the children to put the first sheet to the side and write a number 2 on the back of a second sheet.
- Play the second piece of music and repeat the process.

- Once you have played all the music and the pupils have created their artwork, ensure all pieces are able to dry.
- When all of the artworks are dry, tape all of the pieces labelled 1 together to create a large mural reflecting the class's feelings about the music. Do the same for each number.

Lesson plan 2 – Small groups/pairs

- Spilt the class into small groups and assign each an emotion.
- Allow them to choose tools and paint colours that they think represent the emotion.
- Working together, ask them to create a piece of art that shows that emotion. Remind them that it doesn't have to be literal; they don't need to draw a face experiencing that emotion.

Extensions

Option 1 – You can discuss with the class the similarities between everyone's art for each piece of music/emotion, how the different music/emotion created different art, and how it made them feel. Thinking about colours in this way, ask your pupils to identify the colours they used, why they chose them, and if they make them feel a specific emotion.

Adaptions

Option 1 – Lay a white sheet stretched out on the ground. The larger canvas allows pupils to use larger tools such as wall rollers and tyres, reducing the need for fine motor skills. They could also use wellies dipped in paint to create footprints, or rollers can be attached to a wheelchair or walker.

Bubble painting

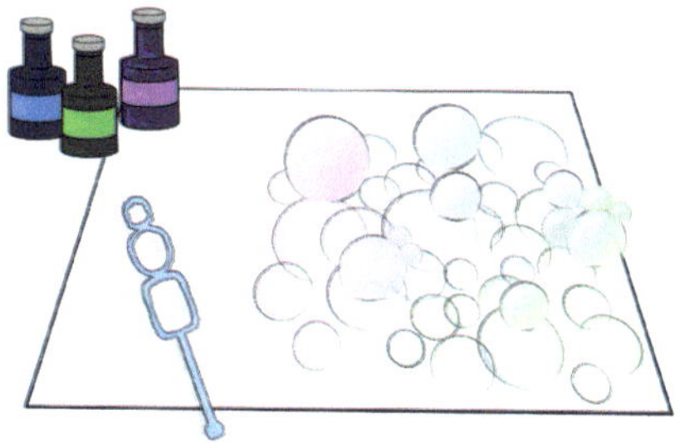

Bubbles are beautiful liquid air pockets that create perfect circles when they pop. When colour is added to bubble mixture, they become a way to create an interesting art piece.

Colour mixing is a key element of art and allows children to experiment past the initial primary colours of red, yellow, and blue. As the bubble mixture remains wet as it lands on the paper, it allows for the colours to mix.

Aims

To create a piece of art using bubbles.

Items needed

- Watercolour paper or card.
- Bubble mixture – washing up liquid (one part) and water (six parts).
- Bubble wands.
- Food colouring/paint.
- Cups or bowls.
- Plastic bottle with the bottom cut off, sock/wipe, elastic band (2).
- Straw (3).

Lesson plan 1 (paint bubbles)

- Add a couple of drops of food colouring to different cups of bubble mixture.
- Using the bubble wands, blow bubbles onto the paper. This will leave individual imprints of the bubbles as they pop on the paper.
- Wash and dry the wands between colours.

Lesson plan 2 (wipe or sock bubbles)

- Cover the cut end of the bottle with a sock or wipe and secure with an elastic band.
- Dip the covered end of the bottle in the bubble mix.
- Blow into the bottle; as you do, lots of small bubbles will come out the covered end and sit on the paper.

- Wait for the bubbles to pop, leaving an imprint on the paper.

Lesson plan 3 (straw bubbles)

- Mix your paint bubbles in a cup or bowl.
- Place one end of the straw into the cup and blow, ensuring children are blowing and not sucking up the liquid.
- Once there are enough bubbles to reach above the rim of the cup, remove the straw.
- Take your piece of paper and gently lay it over the cup; this will pop the bubbles onto the paper, leaving an imprint.
- Repeat with a variety of colours.

Extensions

Option 1 – Experiment with the colours, starting with the primary colours: Yellow, red, and blue. Start by blowing bubbles of two colours onto each other, identify the colour made, and create an equation with coloured pens/pencils to explain it, e.g., red + blue = purple.

Adaptions

Option 1 – A bubble machine can be used to create the artwork, removing the need to blow the bubbles. The machine will need to be cleaned and dried in between colours.

Potato printing

Potatoes can be used for many interesting projects; one of the easiest is as printing tools. By simply cutting a shape and using paint, a print can be made. The simplicity makes it accessible for all ages, but with added tasks it can be extended to provide challenge.

Aims

To create a piece of print artwork using print with potatoes.

Artist: *Andy Warhol*

Andy Warhol's work often featured repeated images with different bright contrasting colours; his style is known as pop art. His artwork often featured the relationship between artistic expression and advertising as seen with the Campbell's Soup Cans or exploring celebrity culture like his Marilyn Diptych. By using bright "popping" colours and repetitive images, pupils can recreate his style with their own images.

Items needed

- Potatoes.
- Knife.
- Cookie cutters.
- Paint.
- Paper.
- Kitchen roll.

Lesson plan

- Cut all of the potatoes in half; each half will be a different print.
- Press a cookie cutter into the flat face of the potato; this will shape the potato into the shape of the cookie cutter.
- Alternatively use a knife to cut the potato into your chosen shape. This can be done by the pupils using a butter knife.
- Dry out the flat face of the potatoes by blotting them on kitchen roll or cloth.

- The potatoes can then be used by dipping the flat side into paint and then onto the paper. Using different shapes, the children can create images.

Extensions

Option 1 – On a fresh piece of paper, draw a grid splitting it into six squares. Using the potato prints, create the same image on each of the squares. Try changing the colours so each image has the same shape but different colours.

Adaptions

Option 1 – For children who struggle to maintain grip on the potato, you can add a fork stuck into the back, which can be used as a handle for the potato printing.

Option 2 – Provide an outline of a picture that contains the shapes of the cookie cut potatoes. The pupils can then match the potato shapes to the picture and choose the colours they use for each of the shapes.

Wax designs

Using wax to repel water can make paper water repellent. Crayons are often used to make paper boats not only colourful but also waterproof! When used in a piece of art, crayon can form clear outlines, as it repels the paint.

Aims

To create a piece of art with wax as a repellent outline and paint filling in the colour.

Artist: *Henry Moore*

Henry used wax resist with ink and watercolour to draw Londoners sheltering from the Blitz during World War 2. He used the wax to create the light and the ink to form the shadows. In some of his images, he also added coloured ink as additional highlights.

Items needed

- White/silver crayons.
- Watercolour paint.
- Paint brushes.
- Paper.

Lesson plan

- Start by drawing an image onto the piece of paper using only the crayon.
- Using the watercolour paints, brush over the crayon covering the whole sheet. Use various colours.
- The crayon will repel the paint, leaving the original image clear with a colourful background and fill from the watercolours.
- The wax resist looks best when there is paint both sides of it.

Extensions

Option 1 – Henry Moore used wax resist to play with light and dark, using the wax to show areas of light then paints and ink to form shape and shadows. Experiment with pressing the crayons harder and lighter, then painting over and looking at which section repels the paint more. Draw a simple shape and choose one side to be light. Try to create a gradient from light to dark across the shape, using the wax for light and paint for dark.

Option 2 – Collect some leaves and place them with the veins facing upwards. Put the paper over the top and create a rubbing of the leaf with the crayon. Paint over the rubbing in the shape of the leaf. The wax veins will repel the paint leaving them exposed.

Adaptions

Option 1 – Print out a colouring-in picture and ask the pupil to trace over the lines with the crayons. They can then paint over the top, and the wax of the crayon will repel the paint from the lines, leaving them clearly identifiable.

Tea staining

Tea stains are often used to make treasure maps and other interesting projects look old and worn. But tea can also be used to create images. The higher the ratio of tea, the darker the stains will be.

Aims

To create a piece of art by finding patterns in tea stains.

Artist: *Dara Gold*

Dara works with tea to create art and was the first person to put Stephen Hawking into a video game! She starts by splotching a wet tea bag onto a page and then uses a marker to create an image following the shape of the tea stains. Using the tea stain shapes as inspiration, Dara creates recognisable illustrations including lots of people and animals.

Items needed

- Tea bags and water.
- Mug.
- Black marker or felt tip.
- Thick paper or card.

Lesson plan

- Place the tea bags in hot water and allow it to cool.
- Let the pupils drip the tea and press the bags onto the paper.
- Once finished, remove the tea bags and allow the paper to dry.
- Once the paper is dry, the tea stains will show clearly, some areas darker than others.
- Looking at the stains, ask the pupils to use the pen to follow any lines or shapes they see.
- Like looking for images in the clouds, pupils should use their imagination to create their art.

Extensions

Option 1 – By using a variety of different teas, including fruit teas, pupils can create tea stains of different colours. Alternatively, add a small amount of food colouring to the tea. Following this the pupils can continue with the lesson adding shapes and images using a pen.

Option 2 – Offer pupils a variety of liquids that can be used to stain the paper. These could include coffee, cranberry juice, or squash. Can they identify which liquid creates the darkest stains and which creates the brightest colours? Pupils could also use sponges to simulate a tea bag. Following this the pupils can continue with the lesson, adding shapes and images using a pen.

Adaptions

Option 1 – Instead of using the tea bags directly on the paper, use a spoon to move the tea onto the paper. Pupils could also use eyedroppers to move the liquid onto the paper.

String painting

String is easy to manoeuvre and can be used as a tool to apply paint or as part of the artwork, making it more three-dimensional. The effect can be changed by using different thicknesses of paint, and the second lesson plan allows for experimenting with symmetry.

Aims

To create a piece of artwork using string.

Artist: *Ben Koracevic*

Ben creates art by winding string around carefully placed nails. The difference in proximity of the nails and string leads to light and shadows. He creates realistic images of animals, people, and cities using only these two materials. By working on a flat surface and adding glue to the paint, pupils can create an image using string, laying it out to form outlines and folding it next to itself to form coloured areas.

Items needed

- String and scissors.
- Card.
- Paper.
- Liquid watercolour paint.
- PVA glue.

Lesson plan 1

- Set up each of the paints in different bowls and add PVA glue.
- Soak a piece of string in the paint ensuring that all of the string is covered. Then remove the string, pulling it gently between two fingers to remove the excess.
- Place the string onto the piece of card, and lay it out in whatever pattern you wish.
- Continue to add pieces of painted string until you have completed your image.
- Leave the piece to dry, and ensure it is kept flat.

Lesson plan 2

- Set up each of the paints in different bowls or pots and allocate a piece of string to each colour.
- Fold your piece of paper in half and then re-open it.
- Choose your first colour and dip the string in; make sure it is completely covered. Then remove the string, pulling it gently between two fingers to remove the excess.
- Place the string onto the side of paper that is flat on the table. You can arrange it in any way, but leave one end off the edge of the paper.
- You can add a second or third piece of string with different colours of paint.
- Fold the piece of paper over and place a hand firmly on top. Using the other hand pull the string out.
- Open up the paper and leave the artwork to dry.

Extensions

Option 1 (lesson plan 2) – Aim to make an image; you will need to lay out the string in a way that when it's replicated on the other side, it will form a full image. A good example might be to create a butterfly.

Adaptions

Option 1 (lesson plan 1) – Provide pupils with a colouring page. They can lay the string along the outlines of the image. Then, colour in the image with coloured pens or pencils before leaving it to dry.

Option 2 (lesson plan 2) – Tape the ends of the string to pencils to create handles. This will make it easier to pull the string out from the paper.

African silhouettes

Art often focusses on the colour and light of objects. This activity uses bright colours of the background to enhance the shape of a silhouette. The savanna is characterised by a mix of grass and woodland featuring some of the most iconic animals, including elephants, lions, and zebras. Due to the open planes, the sunrise and sunset create a stark contrast of the silhouette of animals against the burning sky.

Aims

To create an image of the savanna sunset and silhouettes.

Artist: *Kara Walker*

Kara uses the simplicity of shadows and cut-out shapes to form images and tell stories of history. She has turned some of her pieces into films featuring shadow puppets and title cards set against brightly coloured backgrounds. One of her most famous exhibitions showed black silhouettes cut from paper contrasted against a large, stark, white curved wall.

Items needed

- Coloured pastels.
- White paper.
- Black paper/printed silhouettes of animals.
- Scissors and glue.

Lesson plan

- Start with the white piece of paper and the pastels.
- Create a sunset with a mix of warm colours like yellow, orange, and red. You could leave a white circle for the sun.
- Cut a strip of black paper and stick it to the bottom of the sheet on top of the sunset.

- Cut out the shapes of trees and animals that would be found in the savanna. Pupils could draw their shapes on the black paper with pencil and then follow the lines to cut them out.
- Stick these to the paper with their bases touching or overlapping the black strip already stuck down.

Extensions

Option 1 – Using three pieces of paper or splitting one piece into thirds, ask pupils to think about how the sunset changes as time passes. Each piece of paper should contain the sunset at different time intervals with the sun getting closer to the horizon each time. They should then add the silhouettes of the animals and trees, moving the animals appropriately.

Option 2 – Ask pupils to think of other horizons that could be paired with a brightly coloured background. This could include a city, mountains, or a boat on water. Using a variety of coloured pastels, they can create a bright background; it doesn't have to be realistic like a sunset.

Adaptions

Option 1 – Provide pupils with precut silhouettes of the animals and trees, allow them to stick to their sunset as they wish.

Tissue paper window

Stained glass windows are a prominent feature of many churches and other religious buildings. The technique can also be seen in lamps and other interior decor. They often portray panels of images that make up a story. Stained glass has the unique feature of changing the colour of the light that pours through it. This can be replicated with tissue paper and a clear backing sheet.

Aims

To create an imitation of a stained-glass window.

Artist: *Henri Matisse*

Henri was a talented artist who created art in many forms including paint, sculpture, paper cut-outs, and stained glass. He created artwork by cutting out brightly coloured pieces of paper and layering them to create images. He also used this cutting paper as a way to design his stained-glass pieces.

Items needed

- Tissue paper.
- Scissors.
- Sticky back plastic.
- Black card or paper.
- Felt tip pen.

Lesson plan

- Cut out the chosen shape of the window; this looks best with black card or paper.
- Cut a piece of the sticky back plastic and lay it out on a flat surface like a table. Ensure it is secure and there are no wrinkles.
- Stick the cut-out window on top and cut the excess plastic off.

- Add pieces of tissue paper onto the sticky plastic. You can cut different shapes, or overlap the paper to create new colours and create patterns. The window will look best if the entire surface is covered.
- When complete, take a second sheet of sticky back plastic and carefully lay it over the tissue paper, ensuring there are no wrinkles.
- Cut off the excess plastic and display the piece. Blu Tack works well to stick the piece to a window.
- Watch the light flow through, changing colours.

Extensions

Option 1 – On a piece of paper, the pupil can draw a design of the picture they want to create. They will need to think in block colours and simple shapes. This can then be put underneath the frame and plastic. When creating the frame, ensure the entire image will fit inside. The pupil will then need to fill each section of their image using their chosen colours of tissue paper. They may want to highlight the lines by using a felt tip pen or marker on the tissue paper; this will need to be done carefully to avoid ripping the tissue paper. Once complete, a second piece of sticky back plastic can be added.

Adaptions

Option 1 – Provide pre-cut tissue paper in small pieces or confetti. Allow pupils to pour the confetti over the plastic and shake off the excess. They can then fill in the gaps with the excess.

Skittles patterns

Skittles might make a tasty snack, but they also come in useful for making colourful artwork. The colourings that make up part of the outer shell easily dissolve in water, making interesting patterns.

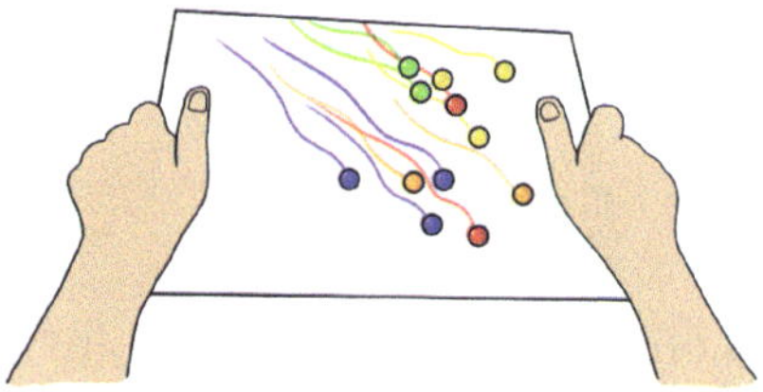

Aims

To create patterns using the food colouring in Skittles.

Artist: *Janet Sobel*

Janet started her art career using scraps of her children's art materials and progressed to work with a variety of mediums. When working she would pour the paint, tip the canvas, and blow the liquid across the page. Her abstract work resulted in paint dripped in splatters and continuous looping lines across the page.

Items needed

- Skittles.
- Water in a jug.
- White plate (1).
- Card and tape (2).

Lesson plan 1

- Set up a white plate on a flat space like a table.
- Arrange the Skittles in a pattern around the edge of the plate.
- Slowly pour the water into the centre of the plate until it reaches past the Skittles. Be careful not to displace the Skittles.
- Watch as the colour seeps out of the Skittles, creating a pattern on the plate.

Lesson plan 2

- Start by taking the piece of card and laying it flat on the table.
- Dip individual Skittles into water and allow them to drip. Transfer the Skittle to the card.
- Continue to add more wet Skittles in a pattern.

- Pick up the card and tip it onto an angle. Watch the Skittles move, leaving a trail of colour behind them.
- Try dropping wet Skittles onto the page and watching them form a splatter.

Extensions

Option 1 – Complete the first lesson plan creating a pattern on a white plate. Following this, take a piece of card, some more Skittles in the same colours, and a small pot of water. By dipping the Skittles into the water, they can then be used as paints. Once wet, move the Skittles across the paper to copy the pattern created on the plate.

Option 2 – For this you will need white sheet or t-shirt cut up into squares for each pupil. Complete the first lesson plan allowing the colour to seep into the middle of the plate. Slowly lay the cloth in over the plate, allowing it to rest in the water and collect the colour. Create multiple plates of colours to add patterns or different areas on the cloth. Remove the cloth and allow it to dry.

Adaptions

Option 1 – For some pupils, it may be difficult to place individual Skittles. Use a cookie cutter to allocate a space on the plate. Add the Skittles into the area confined by the cookie cutter. Add the water to the inner area and lift the cookie cutter slightly to release the colour while keeping the Skittles contained.

Polka dot painting

Polka dots are a popular part of fashion, especially in children's clothing, they are often viewed as something playful. Dots are used exclusively to create some art forms such as pointillism, which involves painting using small dots of a colour that blend to form an image when viewed from a distance.

Aims

To create a piece of art featuring colourful polka dots.

Artist: Yayoi Kusama

Yayoi is a Japanese artist often named the Princess of Polka Dots due to her indulgent use of polka dots in her work. She makes lots of interesting art, including paintings, sculptures, and performances. They all feature bright, bold design choices and, most importantly, polka dots.

Items needed per group

- Paint on plates or trays.
- Round objects e.g., balloons, balls, sponges, Q-Tip's, oranges, buttons.
- Large pieces of paper (you could stick multiple pieces together depending on the group size).
- Paint brushes.
- Pencil.

Lesson plan 1 – Whole class/small groups/pairs

- Each group will need a large piece of paper spread on a flat surface that they can all reach.
- Pupils should start by choosing a round object and dipping it into a colour of paint.
- They should then print the paint onto the paper.
- They should continue to choose different objects and colours until they have covered the majority of the page.

Lesson plan 2 – Individual

- Each individual will need a piece of paper and a pencil to start with. They should draw a simple outline of an image, such as a butterfly, bug, or flower.
- Pupils may want to paint some of the background or the base of the object first. They should choose bright colours.
- Pupils should then choose a round object and dip it into a colour of paint.
- They should then print the paint onto the paper to create the outline and fill the image they have drawn.
- They may also want to add dots to the background.
- They could use a variety of sizes and colours of dots to create a bright and bold piece.

Extensions

Option 1 – Choose a shape other than a circle; find objects that are that shape and then use them to print patterns onto the paper. Pupils should think about an image that would be easier to draw with different shapes; for example using prints of squares could make painting a robot easier.

Adaptions

Option 1 – Tape multiple round items together and dip them into the paint before printing onto the paper. This will create interesting patterns and speed up the process of covering the paper.

Option 2 – Instead of using objects which require being held, pupils can use their fingers to dot the paint onto the page.

Reference List

1. Morriss-Kay, G.M., 2010. The evolution of human artistic creativity. *Journal of Anatomy, 216*(2), pp.158–176.

2. Tambling, P. and Bacon, S., 2023. The arts in Schools: Foundations for the future. Calouste Gulbenkian Foundation. Available at https://www.anewdirection.org.uk/asset/7712.

3. Fudim, S.R., 2024. How the arts benefit the whole child. Whittier Scholars Programme, Whittier College.

4. Coholic, D.A. and Eys, M., 2016. Benefits of an arts-based mindfulness group intervention for vulnerable children. *Child and Adolescent Social Work Journal, 33,* pp.1–13.

5. Lloyd, K., 2017. Benefits of art education: A review of the literature. *Scholarship and Engagement in Education, 1*(1), p.6.

6. Cornock, S., 2003. Celebrating the achievement of the art schools: A new resource. *Fineart. ac. uk.*

7. National curriculum in England: art and design programmes of study – key stages 1 and 2. https://www .gov.uk/government/publications/national-curriculum-in-england-art-and-design-programmes-of-study

Chapter 9
FINE MOTOR SKILLS

From the moment we are born, we begin to learn how to move and control our bodies. Each day, we develop gross motor skills, using large muscles to move the whole body. As we calibrate these bigger movements, the body develops fluidity and automaticity in movement. Meanwhile, we use small muscles to control more specific parts of our body, such as the tongue and lips for producing speech, our eyes, and our hands and fingers to hold objects. Fine motor skills are important for skills such as drawing and handwriting, which is an area of importance in primary school. Alongside fine motor skills, children must develop hand-eye coordination.

The nervous system is made up of the brain, spinal cord, and nerves extending out to all parts of the body. Neurons are nerve cells that send messages across the body, allowing you to breathe, talk, eat, walk, and think. Children are born with billions of neurons, and as they grow, pathways are built, called neural circuits, that act as highways between the different areas of the brain and body [1]. Imagine a baby lying on their back, thrashing for a toy hung above them. Each movement is a message passed through the neurons to create movement. But the baby doesn't always manage to reach the toy. When the baby does touch the toy, their brain begins to identify which of the messages it sent achieved the desired action. The act of neuron pruning is what happens to the neurons that are not needed; they are removed from that message. Over time, the baby reaches the toy more and more consistently, reinforcing the necessary neuron pathway [2].

Most of a child's gross motor skills develop naturally following a broad pattern of developmental milestones, which are reached as children explore the world through exploration and play. Learning is accelerated by watching, interacting with, and mimicking the adults and children they encounter daily.

Many fine motor skills, such as those relating to sight and speech, develop naturally for most children. Some children with developmental delays may require specific instruction on moving their tongue and lips to create recognisable speech sounds. Other fine motor skills, like handwriting, are more complex and require conscious direct instruction and practice.

DOI: 10.4324/9781003515234-10

Humans are believed to have been writing for nearly 6000 years [3], a relatively short time in evolution, meaning the process is nowhere near automatic in the brain. While writing with pen and paper may be what we traditionally consider writing, it is important to note the development of technology and the continued need for fine motor skills in learning to type or other communication methods, such as sign language.

Beyond the fundamentals of dressing and eating, these activities aid in cultivating a wide spectrum of abilities that benefit everyday tasks. Think about how we might thread a needle, or the precise movements needed to tie shoelaces; these activities not only enhance fine motor skills but also promote patience, focus, and the ability to follow complex instructions.

Furthermore, engaging in activities that develop fine motor skills can have a direct impact on academic learning. For instance, the improved dexterity and control gained can enhance a child's ability to write neatly, draw detailed pictures, and manipulate small objects, such as counting beads or assembling puzzles. These skills are crucial not only for academic success but also for fostering creativity and problem-solving abilities. The intentional practice of these skills also supports cognitive development. As children concentrate on completing tasks that require fine motor skills, they are also learning to process instructions, remember sequences, and solve problems. This cognitive engagement is vital for academic achievements and can be seen in various subjects that require meticulous handwork, such as science experiments or art projects.

In summary, the development of fine motor skills through various activities is not just about mastering the ability to perform tasks like buttoning a shirt or using cutlery efficiently but also about laying a strong foundation for physical, cognitive, and academic growth. These skills extend far beyond the classroom, preparing children for the intricate demands of daily life and helping them to become more independent, capable, and confident individuals.

Activities included in this chapter

Activity	Whole class	Groups	Pairs	Individuals	Extensions	Adaptions
Chopstick challenge						
Mushy monsters						
Finger twister						
Giant sewing						
Newspaper collage						
Spaghetti excavation						
Origami boats						
Make a puzzle						
Paper flute						
Flower crown						

Chopstick challenge

Chopsticks are simple utensils used widely across Asia to eat. They have a longstanding history in China and are the traditional way to handle food. Chopsticks require the user to engage their fine motor skills and can be the base for many fun activities.

Aims

To use chopsticks to move an item.

Items needed per group

- Chopsticks, one pair per person.
- Items to move, e.g., sponge, pasta, pom poms, marshmallows

Lesson plan 1 – Whole class/small groups

- If pupils are not familiar with using chopsticks, there are lots of videos and instructions available online.
- Sit the pupils in a circle. Each child will need a pair of chopsticks (or a few pairs of chopsticks that can be passed on ahead of the object).
- One pupil will need to start with an object. A soft item like a large marshmallow will be easiest, while a hard item like pasta will be more difficult.
- The aim is for the pupils to pass the item around the circle, with it only touching chopsticks. It cannot touch the floor or their hands.
- If the item falls, the circle resets at the pupil that dropped it. To complete the game, the item must make it back to the last place it fell or touched someone's hand/the floor.
- Set a timer to see how fast the class can work together to get the item around the circle. Or split the class into teams of the same size and race to see which team can move the item around their circle the fastest.

Lesson plan 2 – Small groups/pairs/individuals

- Set up two or more trays or pots. One should be filled with items to be sorted. There should be enough pots for all of the items to be separated into categories.

- The pupils can work alone or in pairs/teams to sort the items into their pots.
- They can only use chopsticks to touch the items.
- Pupils could race against each other or a timer to see who can move the items the fastest.

Extensions

Option 1 – Change the items to be moved to items that are smooth and harder to grip, such as grapes or mini eggs.

Adaptions

Option 1 – Chopsticks can be difficult to use and hold, so alternative chopsticks can be used which are connected at the top, ensuring the sticks don't fall apart. Alternatively, pupils could use tweezers or kitchen tongs.

Option 2 – Change the items to a mouldable substance such as playdough. When gripped with the chopsticks, the playdough will mould, making it easier to pick up.

Mushy monsters

Making shapes in playdough uses lots of fine motor skills. Making mushy monsters is a great place to start. The soft dough provides a tactile experience with lots of proprioceptive feedback, strengthening the hands and fingers. Pupils can complete a variety of actions, including rolling, squishing, moulding, and flattening, among others.

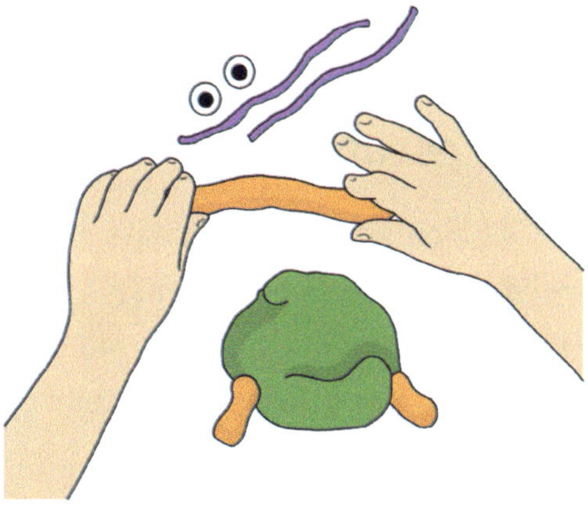

Aims

To create a monster using playdough.

Items needed per group

- Playdough/saltdough.
- Pipe cleaners, beads, buttons, pasta, googley eyes.
- Paper and pens (2).

Lesson plan 1 – Individual

- Challenge the pupils to create a monster using the playdough.
- They can add other items to make the monsters, such as googley eyes, pipe cleaner legs, or a button nose.
- Encourage them to add lots of different features that make their monster interesting.
- They could make lots of monsters having a party or a family of monsters.

Lesson plan 2 – Small groups/pairs

- Each pupil will need a piece of paper and some coloured pens or pencils to start with.
- Ask each pupil to draw a monster using lots of different shapes and the objects available.
- When they have finished drawing, the pupils will need to swap drawings with one of their peers.
- The challenge is then to build the monster that their peer drew, using the colours and materials shown in the drawing.

- When they have finished building, they should compare their models with the drawing and talk to their peers about what they did well and what things are different to the drawing.

Lesson plan 3 – Whole class/small groups

- As a class or group, create a list of body parts for a monster.
- Split the class into teams.
- Give each team some playdough and a mat or tray to build on. They will need to be in a line or circle so that each child can pass the playdough onto the next child.
- One by one, each child builds only one body part. For example, the first child makes the head, the second the eyes, and so on.
- When each child finishes their body part, they should pass it and the materials onto the next person.
- Timers could be set to limit how long each pupil gets the playdough, or the teams race to see who can finish first while still making the best monster.

Extensions

Option 1 – Give the pupils an additional challenge by saying they can only use one hand to make the monsters or that they have to build using a fork and knife. In addition to using their fine motor skills to hold the cutlery, it will also work on their hand eye coordination.

Adaptions

Option 1 – Provide pupils with simple images of monsters built from simple shapes that can be replicated with playdough.

Finger twister

Twister involves contorting your body and getting tangled up trying to reach the different colours. This activity follows a similar vein but only uses your fingers. It encourages children to separate the control and movement of each of their fingers.

Aims

To follow instructions and independently move each of your fingers.

Items needed per group

- Paper.
- Coloured pens/pencils.
- Two dice (1).
- Masking tape (1).

Lesson plan 1 – Small groups/pairs

- Draw a simple grid on a piece of paper, 6 by 4.
- Colour a circle in each grid square. A traditional twister mat has four columns, one of each colour.
- Add a piece of masking tape onto each side of both dice.
- On one dice add the colours on the twister board. On the second dice add the number of the fingers, 1 being the thumb and 5 being the little finger. You will need to repeat two of the colours and one of the fingers.
- The pupils should take it in turns to roll the dice and place the finger on the colour rolled. They will need to choose one hand to play with and then swap hands for a second game.
- The game continues as the pupils add different fingers onto the board.

Lesson plan 2 – Small groups/pairs/individuals

- Each pupil will need to draw a simple grid on a piece of paper, 6 by 4.
- Colour a circle in each grid square. A traditional twister mat has four columns, one of each colour.

- Each pupil should draw around each of their hands, labelling them left and right.
- Colour in the tips of each finger with the different colours of the twister grid.
- Once each pupil has two hands with coloured fingers, those in a group or pair should swap their hands with a peer.
- Their challenge is then to try and match their fingers to the colours assigned on the drawing.

Extensions

Option 1 (lesson plan 1) – limit the pupils so that they cannot share a dot, or each dot can only have one finger touching it.

Adaptions

Option 1 – Instead of making the board with four colours, reduce this to two colours, and put the colours in every other column. This will allow pupils to reach the colours more easily.

Giant sewing

Each of the parts of this activity works to build fine motor skills, including drawing, cutting, and sewing. Joining each of these actions together, each pupil can make themselves a multi-material image that is tactile when complete, allowing them to feel the outline of their image.

Aims

To sew a line or shape using string in card.

Items needed per group

- Card.
- Hole punch.
- Pen.
- Scissors.
- String or wool.
- Needle replacement, e.g., hair grip, skewer, knitting needle.

Lesson plan – Individual

- On the piece of card, pupils will start by drawing a large shape. This could be anything from an alien to a flower. It should be relatively simple and not have lots of sharp corners.
- Next, use the scissors to cut out the outline of the shape.
- Using the hole punch, they will need to punch holes along the edge of the shape. Be careful to make sure the holes are not right on the edge of the card. It works best if you only use one side of the hole punch.
- Cut a length of string that is the longer than the circumference of the shape.
- Tape one end of the string to the back of the card.
- Attach the other end to the needle. You may want to add tape to ensure it stays in place.
- Using the needle, loop the string through each of the holes going back and forth through the card.
- To create a solid line of string, you will need to double back to fill in the gaps.

- When the whole shape outline has been covered, cut the string and tape it to the back of the card.
- Pupils can then draw and colour to fill in the centre of their image, for example giving the alien a face or colouring in the flower.

Extensions

Option 1 – Starting with a plain piece of card, pupils can use the hole punch to create a more interesting pattern than just an outline. They will have to be careful to ensure the holes are not over the edge of the card. They can create squiggles or zig zags which can then be sewn with the string.

Adaptions

Option 1 – Fold a sheet of A4 card into strips over and under creating a zig zag shape. Punch holes in the folded card and then unfold to create a straight line of holes which can be used to sew with. An extension of this would be to create square images only such as robots and hole punching normally along the straight edges.

Newspaper collage

Newspapers are full of images containing different colours that can be used to create a collage. Using scissors is a key fine motor skill that requires good hand eye coordination. Pupils will need to find the colours they want within the newspaper and then carefully cut out the shapes with the scissors.

Aims

To create an image using cuttings from a newspaper.

Items needed per group

- Newspapers.
- Scissors.
- Glue.
- Paper.
- Pen/pencil.

Lesson plan 1 – Whole class/small groups/pairs/individuals

- Pupils will need to start by drawing an image on a piece of paper.
- Looking through the newspaper, they will be able to find lots of pictures with a variety of colours.
- Using the scissors, the pupils can cut out the different colours.
- They will then need to glue the pieces of coloured newspaper onto the image they have drawn.

Lesson plan 2 – Whole class/small groups

- Start by laying out a piece of paper for each pupil across a table with the paper edges touching. On the back of each piece of paper, number the pages so they can be identified and put back in the same places.

- Draw an image across all of the pieces of paper using a think black pen. Each piece of paper will need to have at least some of the outline on it.
- Each pupil then takes a piece of paper and fills in the different sections by glueing on newspaper cuttings.
- They can cut out the different colours from the newspaper to create patterns and shades across their page.
- Once all the pupils have finished their piece of paper, they will need to work together to put the whole piece back together.
- The piece can be taped together to create a giant mural.

Extensions

Option 1 – Instead of just filling each section with one colour from the newspaper, encourage them to find different shades of the colours to create patterns or shading for the image.

Option 2 – Encourage pupils to create a more tactile piece by rolling and scrunching the newspaper and then covering it with the coloured pieces of paper they find.

Adaptions

Option 1 – Provide a printed colouring-in picture for pupils to fill in with the newspaper. In addition, you could provide some pieces of tissue paper or coloured paper for pupils to stick down. While these remove the fine motor practice of using scissors and drawing, there are still fine motor skills required to pick up and stick down the pieces of paper.

Option 2 – Instead of using traditional scissors, there are other types of scissors that are easier to manipulate. Loop scissors are sprung open and by gripping the handles the scissors close. Spring loaded scissors have traditional handles but are sprung open so that the pressure closes the scissors rather than the child trying to open the scissors with their fingers. Pupils could also rip the paper with their hands.

Spaghetti excavation

The use of tweezers requires fine motor skills and builds the muscles in a child's hand. This activity requires hand eye coordination to locate spaghetti and pick it up using the tweezers. The squirmy slippy spaghetti adds a layer of difficulty and fun.

Aims

To pick up items using tweezers.

Items needed per group

- Large tray.
- Soil/dry rice.
- Cooked spaghetti (dyed different colours with food colouring for activity (2)).
- Bowls.
- Tweezers.

Lesson plan 1 – Small groups/pairs/individuals

- Set up a large tray with a layer of damp soil and lay the cooked spaghetti over it. Add another layer of soil on top, hiding the spaghetti.
- Give each pupil a pair of tweezers; giant tweezers will be easier to use.
- Give each pupil a bowl.
- Challenge the pupils to search the soil and collect the spaghetti using only their tweezers. When they find a piece of spaghetti; they should put it into their bowl.
- Turn it into a competition by adding a timer and counting how much spaghetti each pupil collected.

Lesson plan 2 – Small groups

- Dye the cooked spaghetti with food colouring. There should be enough different colours for each pupil in the group.
- Set up a large tray with a layer of damp soil and lay the cooked spaghetti over it. Add another layer of soil on top, hiding the spaghetti.
- Give each pupil a pair of tweezers; giant tweezers will be easier to use.

- Give each pupil a bowl.
- Assign each pupil a colour.
- The game starts like a game of hungry hippos, but pupils can only collect the food in their colour. Using their tweezers, they should hunt for their colour.
- The first to collect all of the spaghetti in their colour wins!

Extensions

Option 1 – To make the activity harder, remove the soil or rice and add oil to the spaghetti. This will make the spaghetti much more slippery, requiring the pupils to concentrate and apply the right amount of pressure to pick it up.

Adaptions

Option 1 – Start with a clean tray without soil or rice and replace the spaghetti with playdough/saltdough worms. These are easier to pick up, as they can be compressed with the tweezers and are less slippery than spaghetti.

Origami boats

Origami is a great fine motor skill with folding and pressing folds of paper. Practicing origami boosts thinking and problem-solving using maths by creating shapes. The activity also results in a final product that the pupils can enjoy.

Aims

To strengthen your understanding of shapes. To listen to and follow instructions.

Items needed per group

- Paper.
- Crayons.
- Sink or washing up bowl filled with water.

Lesson plan – Individual

- Each pupil will need a piece of paper.
- Instructions with images can be found on the internet to support the following instructions.
- Fold the piece of paper in half, connecting the two short edges.
- Turn the paper so the fold is at the top. Fold the left onto the right and press then reopen. You now have a centre line.
- Fold down the top right corner to the centre line creating a triangle. Repeat with the left.
- At the bottom of the paper, fold up one of the flaps to cover the bottom of the triangles.
- Turn the paper over and repeat the above step, folding the bottom flap of paper to match the other side. You have made a paper hat!
- The next step is the hardest to grasp. Pick up the paper and put your thumbs inside of the hat on the centre line. Pull the two sides away from each other, slowly, to create a diamond shape and press the folds along the centre lines.
- Slide one of the flap corners underneath the other on both sides of the diamond.
- Place the paper back on the table with the open section closest to you. Fold the bottom corner of the diamond to the top corner. Press the fold.
- Then turn the paper over and repeat the above step to create a triangle.

- Pick up the paper which should now be in the shape of a triangle. Place your thumbs inside the flap at the bottom and pull the paper apart from the centre line to create a diamond shape. Press the fold.
- Holding the two sides at the top, slowly pull the sides apart to form the final boat! Press the boat against the table to flatten it into shape.
- Colour all of the outside area with the crayons to make it waterproof, including inside the base.
- Place your finger into the base of the boat to open it slightly. With your other hand, open up the top of the boat.
- Take your boats to the water and let them float.

Extensions

Option 1 – Pupils should use the internet to find a simple origami project. Then should learn how to create the origami item. Once they are confident following the instructions, pupils should pair up or work with a small group to teach them how to make the origami piece.

Adaptions

Option 1 – Follow the instructions to make a paper hat and decorate it with the crayons. Pull apart the bottom and place gently on your head.

Make a puzzle

Puzzles develop memory and planning skills, as well as giving children time to test ideas and solve problems. Fine motor skills are involved in the drawing and cutting while creating the puzzle as well as picking up and placing the pieces when completing the puzzle.

Aims

To create a puzzle. To improve problem-solving skills through trial and error.

Items needed per group

- Scissors/craft knife.
- Cardboard.
- Paper.
- Glue.
- Ruler.
- Coloured pens and pencils.

Lesson plan 1 – Small groups/pairs/individuals

- Each group will need to start with a piece of paper and coloured pens.
- The first step is to draw an image and colour it in as the final picture for the jigsaw.
- Cut a piece of cardboard the size of the piece of paper.
- Stick the paper onto one side of the cardboard. Press a ruler along the paper to ensure it is stuck securely and flat to the cardboard.
- Turn the cardboard over. Using the ruler and a pen, draw a grid on the cardboard. The smaller the squares on the grid, the harder the puzzle will be. Pupils could also experiment by creating different shapes.
- When the grid is finished, pupils will need to cut out the puzzle following the lines.
- When the pupils have finished their puzzles, they can swap with another group and try to complete the puzzles.

Lesson plan 2 – Small groups/pairs/individuals

- Fold the paper in half three times. Reopen it and use the ruler to mark the lines.
- Draw a line to cut each rectangle in half; this could be a wobbly or zig zay line.
- Draw a picture in each half of each rectangle; these should be connecting images such as opposites, upper- and lower-case letters, letter sound and image of the item including sound, numbers, and amounts, and young and old animals.
- Stick the paper onto one side of the cardboard. Press a ruler along the paper to ensure it is stuck securely and flat to the cardboard.
- Pupils will then need to cut the rectangles out and cut them in half, following the lines that have been drawn on the paper.
- When the pupils have finished their puzzles, they can swap with another group and try to complete the puzzles.

Extensions

Option 1 (lesson plan 1) – Encourage pupils to create a puzzle with different shapes and sizes of pieces. Once they have completed the puzzle with the image facing up, ask them to turn all of the pieces over to be face down. By looking at the shapes and the edges of the pieces, the pupils can try and put the puzzle back together without seeing the image.

Adaptions

Option 1 – Instead of asking the pupils to draw their own images, print out a picture for them to colour in. Alternatively, print out an image that can be stuck to the cardboard straight away.

Paper flute

Playing a musical instrument is a workout for a child's fingers and hands requiring dexterity, strength, and control. This activity engages pupils by asking them to make their own musical instrument before getting the chance to play it. Each step requires different fine motor skills, from cutting the paper and stretching the elastic band to creating the holes and decorating the flute.

Aims

To create an instrument using recycled materials. To play a musical instrument that you have made.

Items needed per group

- Empty toilet roll.
- Greaseproof paper.
- Elastic bands.
- Sharp pencil.
- Colouring pens/paint.
- Scissors.
- Masking tape.
- Paper cup.

Lesson plan – Individual

- Each pupil will need to start with a toilet roll. Using the pens and paint, they should decorate their flute with different colours and patterns.
- Using the sharp pencil, create three holes down one side of the toilet roll. Try and avoid punching the hole on the join. Leave about 1 cm between each hole.
- Cut a circle of greaseproof paper that is bigger than the end of the toilet roll.
- Place the paper over the end of the toilet roll and attach it using the elastic bands.
- To make the paper flute louder, you can cut a hole in the bottom of a paper cup and insert the end of the toilet roll. This can be secured using tape.

- The flute is now complete. To make sounds, hum or ahh into the end of the flute. By placing their fingers over the holes in the toilet roll flute, pupils can experiment with making different sounds.
- Encourage them to try using both hands and different fingers to cover the holes.
- Working in pairs or groups, pupils could also try to create a song that could be performed to their peers.

Extensions

Option 1 – Ask pupils to research different wind instruments and identify the key features of the instruments. Using this information, how might they adapt their paper flute? This could include testing with a different number of holes, adding a mouthpiece, or changing the shape.

Option 2 – This version of a wind instrument is made using a cardboard tube; however it is not the only material that could be used. Pupils should experiment with different materials such as plastic or paper to create different sounds. They could even try to build a tube with holes using Lego and then add a mouthpiece to turn it into an instrument.

Adaptions

Option 1 – Create a pan flute. Lay out a piece of Sellotape. Cut some straws into decreasing lengths and stick them to the tape with the tops all at the same height. Add a second piece of tape on the other side to secure the straws. Blow into the top of the straws to hear the different pitches.

Flower crowns

Many children will have come across the idea of daisy chains. This activity takes the flower chain to the next level by creating a crown or curtain. Pupils can work together or on their own to collect flowers and then braid them together to create something beautiful.

Aims

To create a feature using flowers. To practice tying knots or braiding.

Items needed per group

- Area with lots of flowers (fake flowers can be used).
- String.

Lesson plan 1 – Pairs/individuals

- Start by picking a variety of flowers with long stems; the longer the stems the easier the braiding will be.
- Strip off the leaves to leave a plain stem.
- Choose three flowers with long strong stems, place them next to each other, and pinch together with one of your hands.
- Using the second hand or working with a partner, braid the stems together. This is done by folding the outer stem on the left-hand side into the middle, then taking the outer stem onto the right side and folding it into the middle. Be careful not to break the stems.
- Continue until a short braid has been made.
- Add in a fourth flower. To continue the braid, move the stem with one already included in the braid.
- Slowly add more stems and flowers to thicken the braid until it is long enough to fit around your head.

Another method of connecting the flowers is threading. This can be used on its own to create a bracelet or crown, or it can be used in addition to braiding to add more flowers to the crown.

- Start with one flower; using a fingernail create a slit in the stem near the flower.
- Take a second flower and thread the stem through the slit.
- Create a slit in the second flower's stem just below the join, and thread a third flower through this slit.
- Continue to add more flowers by adding slits into the flower stems.
- To finish the crown or bracelet, attach a flower with a long stem to the end and then feed it back through near the beginning of the chain.
- You may want to tie off sections with the string to ensure it stays together for longer.

Lesson plan 2 – Whole class/small groups

- Find a long stick or pole and tie multiple long pieces of string to the stick with gaps inbetween each piece of string; let the string hang down from the stick.
- Encourage the children to go and collect flowers and leaves.
- Each child can then attach their flowers and leaves to the string by tying them on.
- By adding lots of leaves and flowers to the strings, the pupils can create a beautiful flower curtain.

Adaptions

Option 1 (lesson plan 1) – Wrap a piece of Sellotape around the child's wrist, with the sticky side facing outwards. Ensure the tape is not too tight. The child can then pick the flowers and stick them to the tape, creating a flower bracelet.

Option 2 (lesson plan 2) – Offer the children pieces of tape to use to stick the flowers and leaves to the string.

Reference List

1. Basics, B., 2019. The life and death of a Neuron. National Institute of neurological disorders and stroke. Available at: https://www.ninds.nih.gov/health-information/public-education/brain-basics/brain-basics-life-and-death-neuron.

2. Schuldiner, O. and Yaron, A., 2015. Mechanisms of developmental neurite pruning. *Cellular and Molecular Life Sciences*, *72*, pp.101–119.

3. Fischer, S.R. and Fischer, S.R., 2003. *History of writing.* London: Reaktion Books.

Chapter 10
FOOD

This chapter explores the integration of food-related activities into educational settings, aiming to enhance children's understanding and appreciation of food. Through a variety of hands-on experiences, including sensory exploration and simple cooking endeavours, it encourages young learners to try new foods, recognise diverse flavours and textures, and develop fundamental kitchen skills. By working individually, in pairs, or in groups, children are invited to partake in exercises designed to educate and ensure their safety in the kitchen.

Learning about food is not restricted to cooking meals that can then be eaten by the end of the class; this chapter guides children to explore the sensory dimensions of food, including taste and texture, in an innovative and inclusive manner. Additionally, the chapter touches upon the significant aspect of food presentation through activities aimed at making meals visually appealing, fostering an approach to food education that encompasses both nutritional and aesthetical considerations.

Integrating food-related activities into the curriculum has a wide range of educational benefits. These can include fostering teamwork and collaboration, enhancing fine motor skills, encouraging problem-solving and decision-making, and promoting language development through discussions about food. This chapter equips educators and parents with the tools to create meaningful and enjoyable food experiences, ultimately promoting a positive and open-minded food culture among children.

Learning to cook has been a highly debated topic for a long time, from debates over whether lack of skill in cooking is the reason for a lack of health and nutrition in poor communities to the gender bias of household tasks, including child-rearing and supplying family meals [1]. The inclusion of food education in schools generally reflects society's views on the topic; in modern times, all pupils take part in lessons focussed on food, with the importance of health and nutrition being a central theme alongside competency in using various kinds of kitchen equipment.

An underlying theme of this chapter is teaching children that no food is bad food. This is also highlighted in the "Health and our bodies" chapter, with an activity looking at what makes

DOI: 10.4324/9781003515234-11

a healthy diet using the Eatwell food plate. It is important to understand the psychological effects of food shaming and how to avoid it when teaching children about food, especially young girls; by the age of 12, they can be subject to negotiations around belonging and body shaming, affecting their mental well-being and self-concept for a long time [2]. This can be exacerbated by the discussion about the rising rates of obesity and the impact of community and national initiatives to tackle it.

While children are growing up, it is crucial to develop intercultural skills, as intergroup attitudes are strongly influenced by social context; this allows children to slowly learn how to acknowledge and take on other people's perspectives [3]. We must acknowledge the importance of learning about the different kinds of food and the places they come from as a part of this development. Pupils may have experienced foods originating in other countries in restaurants or takeaways, but we also want to teach them about the cultures and traditions these foods hold.

Furthermore, we can acknowledge how children's habits around food can influence their behaviours later in life, including their understanding of their role in environmental stewardship [4]. It is important for children to understand sustainable eating practices and the impact of food choices on the environment. This chapter of activities works to improve pupils' knowledge by guiding them to learn about where their food comes from and how it is grown, in addition to learning about what happens to the food that is not consumed.

In conclusion, this chapter presents a comprehensive approach to integrating food-related activities within educational contexts. It not only aims to foster a deep appreciation and understanding of food among children but also builds crucial life skills such as teamwork, problem-solving, and environmental stewardship. As educators and parents, creating engaging, sensory-rich food experiences is essential to promoting a healthy, inclusive, and curious perspective towards food. This approach nurtures not only a child's ability to enjoy and prepare food but also cultivates an understanding of nutrition, culture, and sustainable practices that will serve them throughout their lives.

Note

Before starting any activity that involves touching or consuming food with your class:

- Ensure they do not have any allergies to the ingredients.
- Ensure the countertop is accessible; this may mean preparing food on a table rather than the kitchen counter or providing a safe step.
- Ensure the children are supervised using any heat, electric equipment, or knives.
- If the situation is unsafe, stop immediately.

Every good food activity starts by washing your hands! It is also a good idea to talk through the process with your class. When you have finished, pupils can discuss what they found easy or hard and rate the food they have made or tasted. With young pupils, it's important to ensure they take part in cleaning up after making food, even if this is just moving utensils to the sink or wiping down the surfaces. Older pupils should be able to set up their workstations and clear up any mess they make.

Progress in line with the National Curriculum [5]

KS1 – *Use the basic principles of a healthy and varied diet to prepare dishes. Understand where food comes from.*

KS2 – *Use the basic principles of a healthy and varied diet to prepare dishes. Prepare and cook a variety of savoury dishes using a range of cooking techniques. Understand seasonality and know where and how a variety of ingredients are grown, reared, caught and processed.*

Elements of this topic are also covered in the "Health and our bodies" chapter.

Activities included in this chapter

Activity	Whole class	Groups	Pairs	Individuals	Extensions	Adaptions
Sensory rainbow						
That looks disgusting!						
Where does it grow?						
When does it grow?						
Alphabet foods						
Cultural meals						
Food waste						
Recycle it!						
Fruit rainbow						
Flatbread pizza						

Sensory rainbow

Children often find it difficult to try new foods, especially when they are mixed together. This activity gives pupils an opportunity to try new flavours and textures without the expectation or pressure of hunger and the need to eat a meal.

Aims

To try a food and identify its flavour or texture.

Items needed per group

- Variety of coloured food; all food should be edible at the time of the activity, e.g., rice should be cooked.
- Plates.
- Spoons.
- Paper and pens.
- Blindfold (2).

Lesson plan 1 – Small groups/pairs/individuals

- Choose a variety of food that is all the same colour, for example, for red: Tomatoes, strawberries, red lentils, ketchup, strawberry jam, kidney beans.
- Set out multiple plates, each with a different food on each plate.
- Provide spoons to explore each of them.
- Encourage the children to try the different foods and think about the different tastes and textures.
- Each pupil will need a piece of paper oriented to landscape. Along the top, they should write or draw the different foods.
- Down the left-hand side, write "taste", "texture", and "/10".
- After trying each food, they should think of one word to describe the taste, another for texture, and then give it a score out of 10.
- Pupils can then take some time to compare their answers with their peers. Are there any foods that everyone described the same or foods that everyone disliked?

Lesson plan 2 – Pairs

- One pupil will need to be wearing a blindfold. The second pupil will choose two foods.
- Pupil 2 will need to provide the food one at a time to pupil 1. This could be by guiding them to pick up a spoon with the food on or guiding their hand to a piece of food that can be picked up.
- Pupil 1 tastes each of the foods and tries to guess what the food is. If they can, identify a feature of the food that made them think of that food. For example, they think it's a grape because it was small and round.
- Pupil 2 should write or draw the guesses on a piece of paper.
- Once finished, pupil 1 can take off the blindfold and look at the foods to see if they were correct.
- The pupils can then swap round, and pupil 1 chooses two foods for pupil 2 to guess.

Extensions

Option 1 – The pupils start by choosing one of the foods they have tasted. They should draw or take a picture of their chosen food at the top of a piece of paper and write the name of the food. They should then think about the food they have tasted and write a short paragraph about it, describing the taste and texture and stating whether or not they would recommend others to eat the food.

Adaptions

Option 1 – Provide pupils with visuals of words for taste and texture that can be assigned to the different foods. They can taste the food and then match a picture of the food with the appropriate description.

That looks disgusting!

We don't just choose food by how it tastes but also what it looks like, smells of, or feels like. This activity encourages pupils to make a simple meal and make it look more appetising. This could be a caterpillar sandwich or biscuit dippers.

Pupils can work independently or together to make these snacks.

Aims

To understand what makes people want to eat food. To make a snack look appetising.

Items needed per group

- Round cookie cutter, bread, sandwich fillings, cucumber, carrot, tomato, margarine (1).
- Biscuits, chocolate to melt, sprinkles, marshmallows, and other decorations (2).
- Knife.
- Chopping board.
- Plate.
- Bowl.

Recipe 1 – Caterpillar sandwich

- Lay out an even number of slices of bread. Butter the bread.
- Add the sandwich fillings to one side and place a second piece of bread on top.
- Press down on the top of the sandwich. Place the cookie cutter on the sandwich, not including the crusts. Press down on the cookie cutter to create a round sandwich.
- Remove the mini sandwich and repeat to create more mini sandwiches.
- Line the sandwiches on end, on the plate, to create the body of the caterpillar.
- Cut a small slice off the tomato so it can sit flat on the plate. Place it at one end of the caterpillar.
- Cut the cucumber and carrot into batons to create legs for the caterpillar. Place them on the plate between each of the sandwiches.
- Pupils could also create a face on the tomato.

Recipe 2 – Biscuit dippers

- Break the chocolate into pieces and place it in a microwave safe bowl.
- Melt the chocolate in short bursts, mixing every 10 to 20 seconds.
- Place the sprinkles and other decorations into bowls.
- Take one biscuit and half dip it into the chocolate.
- Let the chocolate drip and then dip the chocolate-covered biscuit into the different decorations.
- Place the biscuit on a plate and repeat with the other biscuits.
- Once the biscuits have all been decorated put them in the fridge to solidify the chocolate.

Extensions

Option 1 (recipe 2) – Pupils could also make the biscuits before decorating them. This way they can choose the shape of the biscuits too.

Where does it grow?

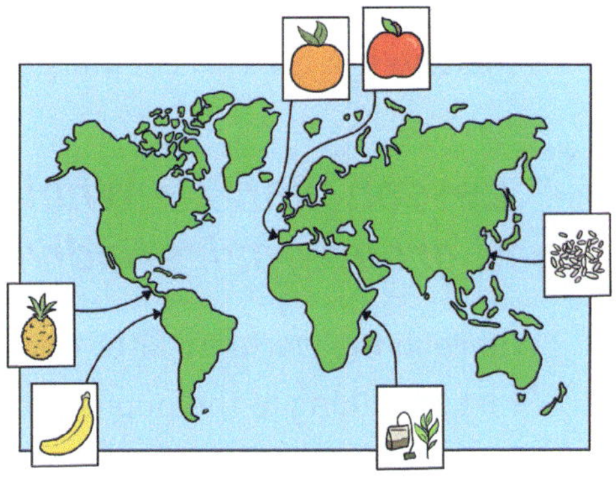

In the modern world, food is often bought from supermarkets with little regard for where it was grown or made. In addition, the convenience of fast food and supermarket food outweighs the need to know its origin. This activity asks pupils to think about where and how their food is grown, or the country from which it originates, and understand more about our food system.

Aims

To identify where different food grows. To understand where our food comes from.

Items needed per group

- Images of tree, vine, bush/on top of the ground, and soil (underground) (1).
- Images of different fruits and vegetables, e.g., carrot, strawberry, lettuce, potato, apple, pumpkin, grapes, tomato (1).
- Scissors and glue.
- Paper.
- Print out of world map per group (2).
- Access to the internet (2).

Lesson plan 1 – Pairs/individuals

- Where do fruits and vegetables grow?
- Start by talking to the pupils about the different fruits and vegetables that they know. Have they ever grown plants themselves? Or have they picked fruits and vegetables themselves?
- Each pair/individual will need both sets of images.
- Start by cutting out all of the pictures and glueing each of the locations in separate corners of the piece of paper.
- Ask pupils to work in their pair/individually to place each of the fruits and vegetables with the location they think they grow.

- Pupils can provide feedback to the class on their thoughts. Discuss each of the fruits and vegetables, ensuring everyone is correct before asking them to stick the fruits and vegetables in the correct place.

Lesson plan 2 – Whole class/ small groups/pairs/individuals

- Where in the world do different fruits grow naturally?
- Start by talking to the pupils about where they get their food, likely the supermarket or maybe a local market. In some cases they might have an allotment or garden where they grow some of their own food.
- Whole class – Each pupil should think of a different food that is grown (fruit, veg, grain) and write or draw a picture of it. Small groups/pairs/individuals – Each should think of around ten foods and write or draw a picture of them.
- They should then find out where in the world the food is grown.
- Pupils will need to locate the country on the map and stick their picture/written word onto the map in the correct location.

Extensions

Option 1 – Ask pupils to choose a few of the foods that are involved in the activity and find out what they need to grow, or how they are made. For example, bananas grow in tropical areas with high temperatures and lots of rain.

When does it grow?

This activity is a great link to a school or community garden, giving pupils time to plan and think about what they would like to grow and how they might do this. Learning when foods grow is important in planning a garden, as you must understand when to plant the seeds. There are also links to knowing which foods are "in season" when buying food at the supermarket.

Aims

To design a vegetable garden. To understand the needs of different plants. To identify when to sow vegetable seeds.

Items needed per group

- Variety of seeds in packets (the back shows a diagram of when to plant and harvest).
- Paper.
- Yearly planner.
- Pen/pencil.

Lesson plan – Whole class/small groups/pairs/individuals

- Each group will need a yearly planner and a plain piece of paper. If you are working as a whole class, put the planner on the board for all to see.
- On the paper, pupils should draw two large rectangles representing the plant beds.
- Talk to the pupils about the weather at the different times of the year. Can they think of which times of the year and the associated weather is important for growing vegetables?
- The task is to choose four different vegetables that can be planted in their garden.
- Pupils will need to decide which plants will go in each bed, when they should be planted, and when they should be harvested.
- They will need to add the timings on their calendar. One way of doing this is to create a key and highlight the time frames in a different colour for each plant.
- Pupils can draw the plants they plan to grow on the paper with the beds.

Extensions

Option 1 – Using the internet, pupils can find out which of the plants grow well together or complement each other. Keep this in mind when planning which vegetables to grow and which should be paired in a bed together.

Option 2 – Pupils should read all of the information on planting the seeds, supported by the internet to find out which seeds should be sown indoors in pots before transferring outside or which seeds need a greenhouse. They could also look at how often the plants need to be watered or fed to pair them more effectively.

Adaptions

Option 1 – Transfer the information from the seed packets to a similar format to the activity. For each seed, create a simplified sheet featuring the yearly planner and highlight the months it can be grown and harvested in. Pupils can then reference these information sheets instead of the seed packets.

Alphabet foods

This activity is a fun game that asks pupils to think about all the foods they know and identify what letter they start with. It encourages them to listen actively to their peers and remember what has been said before adding their own ideas to the game. Pupils also have to keep track of the progress to think of a word starting with the right letter.

Aims

To identify different foods. To work with peers to complete an activity. To listen actively to their peers' input. To develop vocabulary around food.

Items needed per group

- Paper and pen.

Lesson plan – Whole class/small groups/pairs

- Each group/pair will need a piece of paper to record their ideas. This could be done on the board for the whole class.
- Down one side of the paper or in two columns, write the alphabet.
- If completing the activity with the whole class or a group, it is best to sit in a circle so everyone can see each other.
- Go around the circle (or take it in turns in pairs) to think of a food that starts with each letter of the alphabet.
- Pupils can write or draw the food for each letter, or simply remember what they thought of.

For q, u, x, y, and z, there are very limited options – if you are repeating until you run out, these could be considered wildcard or group questions where everyone works together. Alternatively, allow pupils to think of a food that contains the letter/sound somewhere else in the word, not at the beginning.

Extensions

Option 1 – Set a timer and see how quickly pupils can think of a food for every letter. Or with groups/pairs/individuals, race to see who can finish their list first.

Option 2 – Keep going, repeating the alphabet until pupils can no longer think of a food for the next letter that hasn't already been said.

Option 3 (whole class/small group) – Set rules that can disqualify pupils from the game, for example, not saying umm, must say the food within five seconds, or have to draw the food on a whiteboard before the next pupil's turn. All pupils start standing up. Start the game. If pupils break the rules, they must sit down and the game continues but skips them. Continue until only one pupil remains.

Adaptions

Option 1 – Choose a food for each letter of the alphabet and print out pictures. Pupils should cut up a piece of paper into 26 pieces then write a letter on each piece of paper. They can then work together or independently to match the letters with the pictures of the food. They could also write the letters on a piece of paper and stick the matching picture down next to it.

Option 2 – Choose a word such as a month or day or the week. Write the letters down the side of a piece of paper, each letter on a new line. Pupils then think of a food for each letter of the word.

Cultural meals

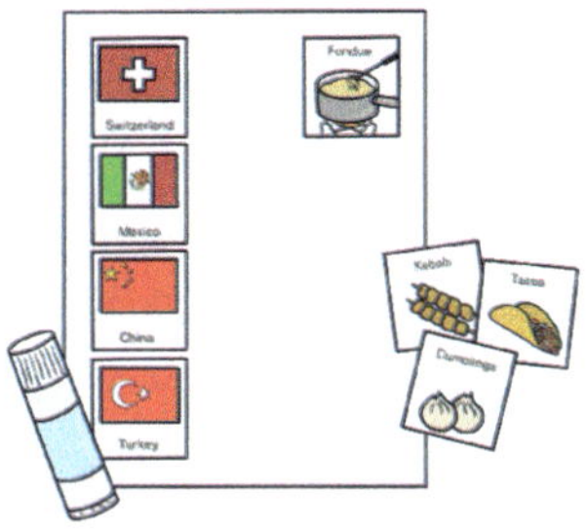

Food is an important part of any culture and is a gateway into more complex discussions around the traditions and celebrations of other countries. This activity encourages pupils to identify foods that are eaten in other countries and the cultural significance they hold to the local people.

Aims

To understand that different cultures eat different foods. To learn about foods from other countries. To describe the foods culturally significant to the different countries.

Items needed per group

- Printed world map (1).
- Images of foods from around the world (1).
- Access to the internet (2).
- Paper (2).
- Coloured pens/pencils (2).

Lesson plan 1 – Whole class/ small groups/pairs/individuals

- Start by talking to the class about the different traditional foods in their household. Are there foods for specific occasions? Have any foods been passed down for many generations? Are there foods specific to their country or religion?
- You can also discuss foods that might be traditional in your area, such as bara brith in Wales, Haggis in Scotland, or the Sunday roast.
- Provide pupils with pictures and names of various foods and a world map. Or this can be done on the board, where everyone can see it.
- Start by letting the pupils guess where they think each food comes from and placing it on that area of the map.
- Encourage them to think of foods they know from other countries and how they might be similar or different.

- Pupils can then use the internet, or you can show the class where each food comes from. You can also discuss the ingredients, any special occasions it is eaten on, and any historical significances.

Lesson plan 1 - Small groups/pairs/individuals/p

- Pupils will need to choose a traditional food from another country. This does not need to be somewhere they are familiar with.
- Using the internet, pupils should look into the origins of the food. They could identify things like where the ingredients are grown, reared or made, the spices used, and the celebration or custom it is associated with.
- They should include a picture of the food on their piece of paper (or in an online document).
- The poster could then show a map of the locations of ingredients or a timeline of the development of the food over the generations.
- They should focus on one element of the chosen food and the country or area in which it is local.

Extensions

Option 1 (lesson plan 1) – Instead of providing pupils with foods, ask them to use the internet to choose ten countries and then research a traditional food from that culture. In addition to finding out what the food is and adding a photo to their map, pupils should look at any other traditions that are done at the same time, for example, if the food is eaten on a special occasion or is eaten using traditional utensils.

Adaptions

Option 1 (lesson plan 1) – Create a matching activity with the origin countries identified; pupils then choose from which of the identified countries the food comes from.

Food waste

Approximately 40% of all food produced for human consumption goes to waste each year, and 60% of this waste is produced at the household level [6]. This activity encourages pupils to think about when they waste food, what happens when they do, and the alternative options.

Aims

To understand that food is wasted. To acknowledge the times when food is wasted at school. To learn about other options for leftover food.

Items needed per group

- Cooking lesson.
- Bins with fresh liners.
- Bin bag.

Lesson plan – Whole class

- This activity is best paired with a standard cooking lesson.
- Before the cooking starts, talk to the class about what they think food waste is. Do they think that they waste lots of food?
- Complete the cooking lesson as normal, but ask pupils to put all food waste into a specific bin and any partially used packets into a specified space. This could include leftover vegetables, bad bits of food that were cut off, extra food that won't be used, and the remainder of any food they don't eat at the end of the lesson.
- At the end of the lesson, group together all of the half-used packets and lay them out in front of the class. Group all of the food waste that was put into the bin. Gather any cooked food that was not eaten at the end of the lesson.
- Looking at the waste at the end of the lesson, can pupils think of anything that can be done to ensure it doesn't all end up in the bin?
- Encourage pupils to discuss how their ideas could be implemented.

Compost – Set up a school composting system where scraps of fruit and vegetables, tea bags, grass cuttings, etc. can be placed. When the compost is made, use it on the school gardens.

Bubble and squeak – Design a meal or a snack using only the leftover food and items that are already in the cupboard, like flour and sugar.

Gifting – Plate up the extra food that has been cooked and offer it to the pupils or teachers from another class.

Grow more – Using the internet, pupils can learn about growing more vegetables from the stems left over; for example, saving the head of lettuce and placing it in water to grow some roots before planting it back in the ground.

Extensions

Option 1 – Write a letter to the headteacher explaining about the high levels of food waste and the solutions they have come up with to reduce waste at the school. These could include whole school initiatives or ideas for the school kitchen.

Option 2 – Design a presentation for another class or assembly for the whole school talking about the issue of food waste and what each pupil can do to reduce food waste in school and at home.

Recycle it!

All food is transported and sold in some kind of packaging; when teaching pupils about cooking and healthy choices, we must also acknowledge the waste created. This activity introduces a fun game of sorting the rubbish to ensure as little as possible ends up in the landfill. The items used in this activity could also be collected and saved for other activities, e.g., the hydration station in "Health and our bodies" or paper flute in "Fine motor skills".

Aims

To understand the importance of recycling. To learn about the different options for rubbish. To learn what items are able to be recycled.

Items needed per group

- Recyclable items.
- Non-recyclable items.
- Compostable items or toy versions of.
- Three open bins or boxes labelled compost, recycling, landfill.
- Bin lid.

Lesson plan – Small groups/pairs

- Talk to pupils about what happens to the packaging in which their food comes and the food that is left over at the end of a meal. Ask them to identify the three places it can end when it leaves their house or the school. These are compost, recycling plants, and landfills. Discuss the impact of sending waste to the landfill and how material like plastic doesn't decompose, it simply gets smaller and ends up finding its way back into our food in animals or our water in the form of microplastics.
- By recycling materials and sending food to be reused in compost, we can reduce the amount of rubbish in landfills. Using your local recycling scheme, you can look up what is allowed to be recycled in your area.
- This game is fun, quick-thinking, and reaction-focussed, encouraging pupils to make swift decisions on where to put different kinds of rubbish.

- Pupil A will need a pile of "rubbish" items, multiple items from each of the three categories.
- A short distance away, set up the bins in a line, with the labels facing pupil B. Pupil B will need to be holding the bin lid.
- Starting slowly, pupil A should throw an item towards the bins. Pupil B will need to catch it on the bin lid and direct it to the correct bin.
- Increasing the speed will make the game harder for pupil B and no doubt cause some laughter as items don't make it into the bins.
- After a set number of items or set amount of time passes, the pupils can swap and try out the other role.
- Once finished, encourage pupils to look at the results and decide if all the choices made were correct.
- End the lesson with a discussion on how they can ensure that the least amount of waste ends up in landfills and what practical changes you can make as a class, such as washing out yoghurt pots to put in the recycling, getting a compost bin for leftover food, or using reusable bottles.

Extensions

Option 1 – Using the local council information on what can be recycled or composted. Ask pupils to make signs or posters to put by the bins around school to encourage other pupils to think about where their rubbish ends up.

Option 2 – Ask pupils to think of ways to make putting items in the recycling more interesting. One idea is to add a basketball hoop to the bins or a target to throw the rubbish at. Pupils could also organise to take bottles to reverse vending machines at a local supermarket to get coupons for school projects.

Adaptions

Option 1 – Instead of throwing the items, have each pupil start with a box of items, and time how long it takes them to sort the rubbish into the correct bins. Or have multiple sets of bins and have pupils race to sort their pile the fastest.

Fruit rainbow

Creating a fruit salad is great practice for chopping food, using fine motor skills and hand strength to control the knife. Pupils can understand and learn about the different types of fruit and talk about the different tastes and textures. Learning to make a fruit salad also provides opportunity to practice peeling and cutting.

Aims

To understand the benefits of eating fruit. To create a healthy snack. To accurately and safely use a knife.

Items needed per group

- Knife.
- Chopping board.
- Variety of fruit in the different colours of the rainbow.
- Plate or bowl.

Method

- Talk to the pupils about the benefits of eating fruit, e.g,. a good source of vitamins and minerals, helps maintain a healthy gut aiding with digestion.
- Clean the fruit.
- Cut up each of the fruit removing seeds and leaves.
- Give each pupil a piece of each fruit to taste.
- Encourage them to try the different fruits and decide which ones they want to include in their fruit rainbow.
- Group the fruit into the different colours.
- If using a plate, start by creating a single line of fruit in each colour in the shape of a rainbow.
- Once all the colours have been added, continue to add fruit to fill out the rainbow.
- If using a bowl, there are two options: A transparent bowl can be filled in layers of the coloured fruit, or an opaque bowl can be filled with a triangle of fruit of in each colour, each group of fruit like a slice in a pizza.

Extensions

Option 1 – Pupils could also pair the fruit salad rainbow with a smoothie. Encourage them to think of fruits that go well together. Using a blender mix some fruit. They should also add some fruit juice, water, or milk to thin down the smoothie. They should think about what colour might be formed when the fruits and liquid are mixed.

Option 2 – Pupils can create shapes in the fruit by slicing the fruit and then using cookie cutters or a knife to create the shapes. They could create an image using the shapes they have created.

Adaptions

Option 1 – Chop the fruit into batons. The pupils can then chop the batons with one hand on the baton and the other hand using the knife.

Option 2 – Print an image of a rainbow and laminate it. Clean the laminated surface. Pupils can then match the different fruit colours to the rainbow and place the fruit on top of the image as a guide.

Flatbread pizza

Flatbread pizza is a simple food to cook but can be the basis of a full meal, making it a great thing for children to learn to cook. The dough required to create flatbread is made up of only three ingredients, which leaves lots of time for pupils to focus on what they want as the toppings, and a chance to practice chopping and spreading.

Aims

To follow step-by-step instructions to create something. To behave appropriately and remain safe in a kitchen. To attempt a range of cooking techniques.

Items needed per group

- Plain flour (350 g).
- Water (150 ml).
- Oil (two tablespoons).
- Seasoning.
- Tomato sauce (or alternative).
- Pizza toppings.
- Oven, large bowl, rolling pin, baking tray, baking paper.

Method

- Preheat the oven to 200 °C.
- Add the flour into a bowl and create a well.
- Add the oil and water into the well.
- Mix well until you have formed a dough; add more flour if it's too sticky, or add more water if it's too dry. As the mixture becomes more like dough, kneed it with your hands.
- Cover the dough and leave it to the side.
- Prep the toppings; these could include cutting pepper, ripping ham pieces, grating cheese.
- Spread some extra flour out on a clean surface. Spread the flour onto the rolling pin.
- Split the dough into four balls. Using the rolling pin, roll each piece into a flat piece. By rotating the dough, you can create a circle, or pupils can create fun shapes.

- Measure and cut out the baking paper to fit onto the baking tray.
- Place the dough onto the baking tray and put in the oven for two minutes.
- Remove the dough bases from the oven and flip them over. You may want to remove the dough from the hot tray by transferring the baking paper onto the surface.
- Spread the sauce over the dough and then add the rest of the toppings.
- Put the dough back on the tray and bake in the oven for eight minutes.

Extensions

Option 1 – Pupils could try creating a stuffed crust. Instead of diving the dough into four, split it into two. The pizza bases can then be stretched. Leave a gap of about 2 cm at the edge of the dough, and then create a circle of cheese or the chosen filling. Fold the outside of the dough over the filling, and press it down with your fingers.

Adaptions

Option 1 – Instead of creating the dough, use premade pizza bases or wraps. For the wraps, only put them in the oven for a few minutes.

Option 2 – Create a set of instructions with visuals to support the words. This ensures pupils can take part with more independence.

Reference List

1. Lang, T. and Caraher, M., 2001. Is there a culinary skills transition? Data and debate from the UK about changes in cooking culture. *Journal of the HEIA*, *8*(2), pp.2–14.

2. Kitching, K., Fernández, E. and Horgan, D., 2022. Sweets are 'my best friend': Belonging, bargains and body-shaming in working class girls' food and health relationships. *Children's Geographies*, *20*(5), pp.590–603.

3. Schwarzenthal, M., Schachner, M.K., Juang, L.P. and Van De Vijver, F.J., 2020. Reaping the benefits of cultural diversity: Classroom cultural diversity climate and students' intercultural competence. *European Journal of Social Psychology*, *50*(2), pp.323–346.

4. Won, S. and Tang, T., 2017. Design for healthy eating: Engaging children to understand food practices. In *A study of the multi-generational relationship with making through mediated designing in collaborative, digital environments*. University of Leeds.

5. National Curriculum in England: design and technology programmes of study. Cooking and Nutrition. https://www.gov.uk/government/publications/national-curriculum-in-england-design-and-technology-programmes-of-study/national-curriculum-in-england-design-and-technology-programmes-of-study#cooking-and-nutrition

6. United Nations Environment Programme, 2024. *Food Waste Index Report 2024. Think Eat Save: Tracking Progress to Halve Global Food Waste.*

Chapter 11

HEALTH AND OUR BODIES

The banner of health and our bodies covers multiple elements. These include relationships, sex, and health education (RSHE), healthy diets or food, and physical education (PE). This chapter teaches children to respect and care for their own bodies and those around them, both physically and mentally. The activities propel the notion that fostering respect and care for one's body and the bodies of others is pivotal, underlining the role of education in instilling these values from a young age.

The text offers practical strategies and actionable educational content for teaching children about staying hydrated and the basics of a balanced diet, which are crucial components of a healthy lifestyle. Learning more about their own bodies and the associated functions expands their physical understanding of health. Giving pupils the information needed to keep themselves healthy supports their autonomy over their own bodies and is integral to improving a child's self-concept. In addition, this can be underpinned by their peers. Our own beliefs about our personality are dynamically shaped by the perception of our body [1]; by creating opportunities for empathy and relationship building between peers, we can support the growth of self-concept.

Pupils' mental health is of utmost importance for their well-being and as a tool in supporting their academic success. Mental health plays a key role in the academic success of an individual, with mental health problems in early childhood and adolescence increasing the risk of poor academic performance [2, 3]. Continuing from the importance of pupils' mental health, developing a supportive environment within schools is critical. Educators and school counsellors play a significant role in recognising early signs of mental health issues and providing the necessary support or referrals. By implementing structured programmes and interventions that promote mental wellness, schools can equip pupils with resilience skills to navigate challenges both in and outside the classroom. The activities in this chapter

DOI: 10.4324/9781003515234-12

open a conversation about creating tools for pupils to use in stressful situations as well as identifying their support network of people they can ask for help.

Furthermore, integrating mental health education into the curriculum can help destigmatise mental health issues among students. This approach fosters an inclusive culture where students feel safe to discuss their feelings and challenges. It's also essential for schools to collaborate with parents and guardians, keeping them informed and involved in the mental health resources and strategies being applied. Peer support programmes can also be beneficial, as they empower students to support each other under supervised guidance. Such programmes not only aid students in need but also build leadership and empathy among the student body.

The chapter emphasises the importance of personal and communal effort in maintaining health, advocating for a supportive and understanding approach towards the well-being of oneself and others. Respecting our peers is an integral part of society and something that often needs explicit teaching through supported play for pupils to fully understand. Studies have shown that peer social acceptance is significantly and positively related to academic achievement [4]. The chapter's activities highlight the importance of consent in building relationships as well as showing compassion and kindness to others. Working through the activities in this chapter will encourage pupils to understand themselves and those around them, support their involvement in the community, and improve their mental health.

Progression in line with the National Curriculum [5]

RSHE – *Understand the role of families and the people who care for them. The characteristics and importance of caring friendships. The importance of respecting others and of self-respect and how this links to their own happiness.*

PE – *Develop fundamental movement skills, becoming increasingly competent in how the body moves individually and extending their skills in cooperation with others. Learn to enjoy communicating and collaborating with each other.*

Food technology – *Understand and apply the principles of a healthy and varied diet.*

The activities in this chapter cover aspects from three areas of the national curriculum: Relationships, sex, and health education; physical education; and food technology. Each of these areas contributes to a child's understanding of their body and how to keep it healthy. In addition, how to connect to their peers is also covered in this chapter.

Activities included in this chapter

Activity	Whole class	Groups	Pairs	Individuals	Extensions	Adaptions
Hydration station						
Food plate						
Where is my...?						
Heart rating						
The five senses						
Consent						
My important people						
Stress wheel						
Compassion cards						
Kindness calendar						

Hydration station

This activity helps children understand why drinking water is important. All living things need water in some form, and humans are no exception. Up to 60% of the adult human body is water; in children, it's up to 75%. Water plays a vital role in keeping our bodies healthy, from being in our blood and transporting nutrients to helping flush out toxins.

Aims

To understand the importance of staying hydrated.

Items needed per group

- Plastic bottle (1).
- Permanent marker (1).
- Craft knife (1).
- Washing up bowl or outside space (1).
- Whiteboards and pens or open space (2).

Lesson plan 1 – Small groups/pairs

- Each group will need a plastic bottle. Their first task is to decorate the bottle. Draw a happy face near the top, a worried face in the middle, and a sad face near the bottom.
- Talk about what things make us thirsty, such as talking, running, going out in the sun.
- Fill the bottle with water and place it over a washing up bowl or take it to an outside space.

(The next step should be done as a demonstration for younger pupils; older pupils will be able to complete it independently with supervision.)

- Poke a hole near the bottom of the bottle with the craft knife for each activity in the day that you think uses water.
- What happens to the water in the bottle? What should we do if we use water during the day? How might you feel if you don't have enough water in your body?

Lesson plan 2 – Whole class

- This is a true or false game.
- Each pupil will need a whiteboard and pen to write their answers on, or this can be a movement activity where an area of the room is assigned "true" and another "false". To answer, the pupils move to the area/answer they believe to be correct.
- Give each statement. Anyone who is incorrect sits out. Those who answer correctly continue to play. Alternatively, you can give pupils points for the correct answer, and those with the most points at the end win.
- Below are some statements about drinking water that could be used:

True	False
Helps your kidneys work correctly	Makes you sleepy
Lubricates and cushions your joints	Helps you float when swimming
Keeps your body temperature normal	Only 20% of your body is made up of water
Helps your body get rid of waster	Drinking water is the only way to hydrate
Only 1% of water on Earth is available for humans	It's impossible to drink too much water

Extensions

Option 1 – Think of ways to stay hydrated that don't involve drinking water; write a list of foods that contain lots of water.

Option 2 – Create a science experiment using two plants to compare what happens when one plant is fed only water and the second is only fed fizzy pop. What difference does it make?

Food plate

The food plate is a common activity involved in learning about healthy eating, often starting by sorting different foods into the categories of the Eatwell plate. This activity takes the learning a step further, encouraging pupils to think about the meals they eat and what they might want to eat.

Aims

To identify the amounts of food needed to form a balanced meal.

Items needed per group

- Eatwell plate.
- Images of two meals.
- Paper.
- Coloured pens/pencils.

Lesson plan 1 – Small groups/pairs/individuals

- First, you will need two images of meals – one could be a lunchbox and the second a hot meal. One will need to have a balanced meal containing roughly the correct percentages to match the sections of the Eatwell plate. The second should have percentages of food that don't match the Eatwell plate. Each pupil will need to be able to see the images.
- Each group/pair/individual will need to look at the meals and create an Eatwell plate that reflects the food shown.
- They will need to include the foods in the meal and think about the percentage of the plate that the food takes up.
- Once finished, they should look at the plates they have drawn and decide if either of them has the right amounts of different foods.

Lesson plan 2 – Pairs/individuals

- This activity involves pupils trying to plan a meal that contains the correct quantities of each type of food as displayed on the Eatwell plate.

- They could choose a school lunch or a meal they eat at home; alternatively, they could search online for a meal that would work.
- Once they have chosen a meal, they will need to create an Eatwell plate containing the ingredients of their chosen meal, showing what item from the meal fits each section of the plate.

Extensions

Option 1 (lesson plan 1) – How could they change the meal to balance it out more like the Eatwell plate? For example, switching a chocolate spread sandwich for a ham sandwich.

Option 2 (lesson plan 2) – Using a computer or tablet, can pupils work out what methods of cooking might make the meal more or less healthy? For example, is it better to deep fry or oven bake chips?

Adaptions

Option 1 (lesson plan 1) – Provide pupils with a blank Eatwell plate that matches each of the meals. It should not have any labels stating which food group goes where but simply already providing the percentages. Give pupils images of the different foods on each plate to be used as manipulatives and placed on the blank Eatwell plates.

Where is my...?

Locating body parts is an easy task, but could you do it blindfolded? The first activity encourages pupils to rely on their knowledge of the locations when they can't see a point of reference. The second activity challenges their knowledge of the organs by pitting them against their peers to think and act quickly.

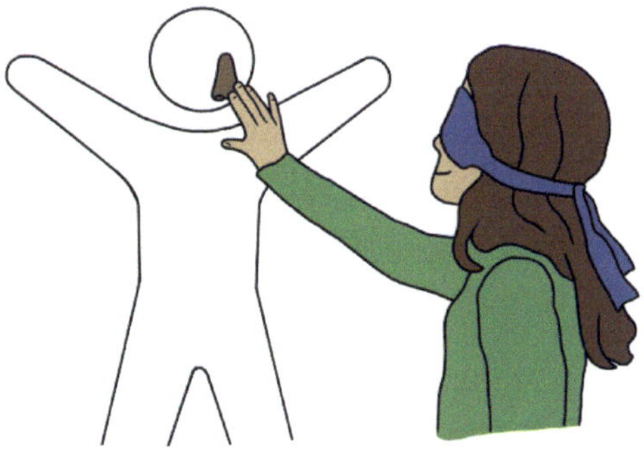

Aims

To correctly locate human body parts and organs.

Items needed per group

- Large outline drawing of a human body.
- Blu Tack.
- Individual body parts cut out (1).
- Blindfold (1).
- Open space (2).
- Individual organs cut out (2).

Lesson plan 1 (body parts) – Small groups/pairs

- Start by sticking the outline of the human body to a wall.
- Pupil A will need to take one of the body parts with a piece of Blu Tack on the back and then put on the blindfold.
- Pupil B will need to slowly spin pupil A around twice until they face back towards the picture of the body.
- Pupil A must then try to place the body part onto the body.
- The pupils can change places and take turns to place the body parts.
- Once finished, they can look at the body and see how many of the body parts they put in the correct place and then move the parts to the correct places.

Lesson plan 2 (organs) – Small groups

- Split the class into teams. Each team will need a body outline and a set of human organ pictures. The game works well if the body outlines are on one wall of a hall or classroom, with space in between to avoid cheating, and the teams are set up with the organ pictures on the other side of the hall or classroom.

- On the start signal, one member of each team will need to grab an organ picture and race to their team's body outline.
- The pupil then places the organ on the body in the place they think it goes.
- The pupils in each team take it in turns until all of the organs have been placed on the body.
- Points can be given for speed and how many organs were placed in the correct area of the body.

Extensions

Option 1 (lesson plan 2) – Provide the pupils with cards that state the purpose of the body part without naming the body part. When they choose a body part, they must also choose the statement that matches and place both onto the body outline as part of the relay.

Adaptions

Option 1 (lesson plan 2) – Give pupils a completed picture of the organs on a body outline; place it in the same place as their body parts. They can then choose a body part, look at the prompt, and remember it as they run to the body outline and place the body part.

Heart rating

This activity gives students a chance to investigate how physical activity effects their heart rate and use their own homemade stethoscope to compare other people's heart rates. Physical activity is an important part of staying healthy. Doing aerobic exercises gets your heart beating faster, which strengthens it and makes it more efficient at delivering blood around the body.

Aims

To learn how to measure and calculate your own and others' heart rates. To understand the effect of physical exercise on heart rate.

Items needed per group

- Cardboard tube from paper towel.
- Funnel.
- Tape.
- Balloon.
- Scissors.
- Stopwatch.
- Paper and pen.

Lesson plan – Whole class/small groups/pairs

- Talk to your class about what the heart does for the body. When you exercise, your body needs more energy, so the heart pumps faster to deliver oxygen more quickly to the areas that need it, like your muscles. As your heart beats, it sends a wave of pressure through your blood. This can be felt in some areas of your body as a pulse.
- Ask each child to try and find their pulse. The easiest place to feel your pulse is by placing two fingers on your neck just below the curve of your jaw. Alternatively, hold out your left hand and raise your thumb; place two fingers of your right hand on your left wrist where it meets the thumb. Pupils may need to try both methods and make slight adjustments to find their pulse.

- To make a stethoscope, start by taping the funnel to the end of the cardboard tube, with the thin section inside the tube. It should look like a plunger when taped together.
- Cut off the small section of the balloon and stretch the rest over the end of the funnel to create a tight surface.
- Take turns gently placing the funnel against someone's chest to listen to their heartbeat. This is a great alternative for children who can't find their pulse.
- To calculate the beats per minute (bpm), set the stopwatch and count how many heartbeats or pulses are felt in 60 seconds. Older pupils could listen for 15 or 30 seconds and then multiply by 4 or 2 respectively. This is your resting heart rate, the heart rate when you are not doing any exercise.
- Set up a circuit of exercises, one for each group or pair (pairs could share stations with others). Each station will need an exercise, a stopwatch, paper, and pen. Activities could include lying on the floor, running on the spot, doing star jumps, sitting in a chair, walking at a normal pace, or hopping on one leg.
- Each pupil will need to create a table on the piece of paper with one column for the name of the activity and a second for the heart rate measured.
- Each group will choose one or two pupils to complete the first exercise, they should do the exercise for one minute.
- Immediately after, they should measure their heart rate or pulse.
- Rotate the pupils around the exercises, taking it in turns until all pupils have a record of their heart rate after completing each activity. They will need a break between activities to return their heart rate to resting. By working in groups or pairs, they can rotate who is completing the activity and who is timing and recording information.
- To complete as a whole class, each activity can be timed and run by the teacher. Leave adequate breaks between activities for heart rates to recover.

The five senses

We use our five senses constantly and often collaboratively. We often rely on our sight more than other senses to identify items around us. These activities encourage pupils to engage their other senses to identify objects.

Aims

To identify an item by actively using your senses.

Items needed per group

- Items for each of the five senses.
- Flash cards or images for each sense (1).
- Blindfold (2).

Lesson plan 1 – Small groups/pairs/individuals

- To see who can find something for each of the senses.
- Each pupil will need to be able to see the visuals for the five senses.
- Set a timer, or challenge your class to race against each other.
- Each group/pair/individual will need to find an item that can be described using one of the five senses.
- They will need to collect five different objects, one for each sense.
- Without labelling the objects, they should then swap objects with their peers.
- Once they have another group's objects, they should try and match the objects to the senses. There will be objects that could be identified using multiple senses.
- Once they have made their guesses, they can discuss with their peers and identify the features of each item and what made them assign it to a specific sense.
- At the end of the activity, take some time to discuss how difficult it is to only use one sense to identify an object.

Lesson plan 2 – Small groups/pairs

- Choose a variety of objects that have a distinctive feature, one for smell, taste, touch, and hearing.

- Pupil A will need to put on the blindfold and place their hands on the table.
- Pupil B will give them each of the items one by one and ensure they try to use only one sense. For example, they will hold an item near pupil A's nose to smell, put some food on a spoon and give it to pupil A to taste, make a noise in front of pupil A, and put an item in pupil A's hands to feel.
- Pupil A should try to guess what each of the items is using one of their senses.
- Once completed, they should remove the blindfold and check if they were correct.

Extensions

Option 1 (lesson plan 2) – To make identifying the item harder, pupils cannot use their hands to touch the object. Pupil A could touch pupil B's arm or the back of their hand with the item. Pupils can talk about where on their body might be easiest to guess what the item is and why.

Adaptions

Option 1 (lesson plan 2) – Let pupil A see the different items before starting, then when they are blindfolded, they can work to match the information from their other senses to the items they have already seen.

Consent

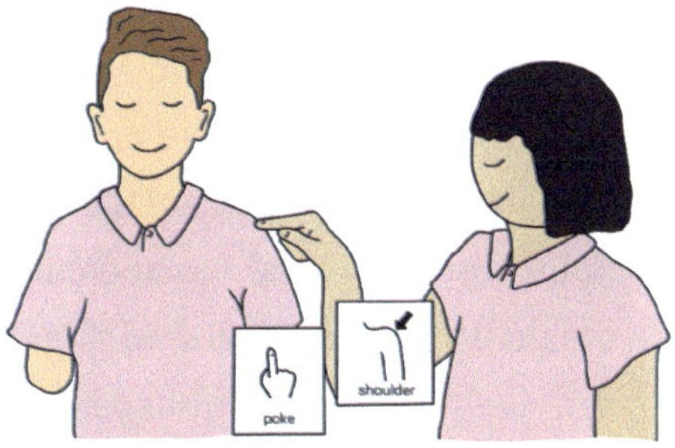

Consent is essential in keeping yourself and others safe; it is an important part of all healthy relationships. It can be seen in how we communicate and respect the boundaries of our friends and strangers. This activity helps children understand the link between permission seeking and physical contact, and supports them in saying no when they are not comfortable completing an action.

Aims

To accurately listen to verbal and observe non-verbal cues of a peer. To respond appropriately to verbal and non-verbal cues.

Books to support learning: *No Means No!* by Jayneen Sanders, *We Listen to Our Bodies* by Lydia Bowers, *Kit and Arlo Find a Way* by Ingrid Laguana and Vanessa Hamilton.

Items needed per group

- Various objects that can be picked up and moved (2).

Lesson plan 1 – Pairs

- Pupils take it in turns to ask their partner a question. The questions can make sense (Can I poke your elbow?) or a little bit silly (Can I headbutt your ankle?).
- The person responding can say "yes", and the action is done.
- Or they can say "no" and offer an alternative. An example of this in life might be: "Can I have a hug?" "No, but you can have a high five". In this game it might be: "Can I poke your elbow?" "No, but you can poke my shoulder".
- Pupils should take the time to listen to their peer's response before completing any action.
- Both pupils should have a chance to ask questions and to answer questions.

Lesson plan 2 – Small groups

Note: This activity may not be suitable for all children due to the need for extensive eye contact.

- Sit around a table and place the objects on the table.
- In the first round, each person needs to say someone's name and ask them to pass one of the objects. If they say "yes" and pass the object, it becomes their turn to ask someone else. If they say "no", the person who asked can try and ask someone else.
- This illustrates it is easiest to communicate when we talk.
- In the second round, no one can talk. Each person needs to try and convince someone else using eye contact and body language to pass an object to them. They can still refuse, though must not speak.
- This illustrates the use of our bodies to send signals of whether or not we consent.
- In the third round, you can only use your eyes, no verbal or physical language. The task is the same to ask someone to pass you an object. They can still refuse, though must not speak or gesture.
- The third round illustrates how hard it is to communicate using eye contact without context.
- You can set a timer for each round to limit how long it continues.

Extensions

Option 1 – Pupils can work in pairs or groups to create a role-play situation to show their peers. This should involve two versions of the same scenario. The first should show one person saying "no" and the other(s) ignoring the boundary that has been set. The second should show one person saying "no" and the other(s) respecting the boundary and adjusting the situation.

Adaptions

Option 1 – Use dice to choose body parts and actions by writing on masking tape on each side or have a set of flashcards for the body parts and actions, and place them face down to choose from.

My important people

It's important that children know who they can talk to if they are feeling upset or overwhelmed or if they need support and advice. This activity asks them to think of people they might talk to in different situations. It can then be used as a map when they are struggling.

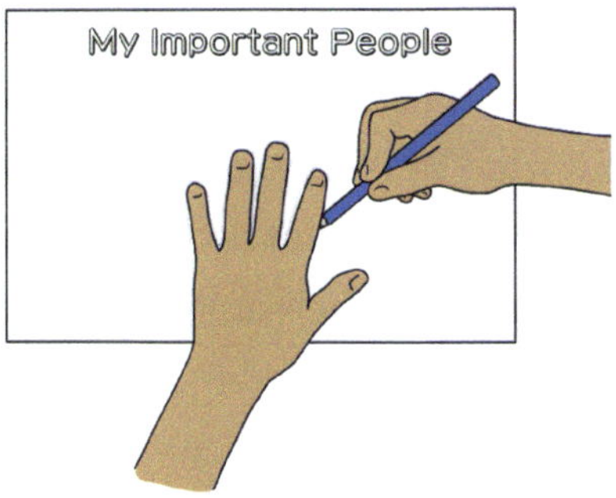

Aims

To identify key people who can help you.

Items needed per group

- Paper.
- Coloured pens/pencils.
- A3 paper (2).

Lesson plan 1 – Individual

- Talk to the class about the people that help them; this could be family, friends, teachers, neighbours, people that run afterschool clubs, healthcare professionals. Who do they go to if they are upset? Who can help them if they are scared? Who would they tell if they had good news? Who would be able to help them?
- Each pupil will need a piece of paper and pen.
- Place a hand in the centre of the paper and carefully trace around it.
- On the finger of each hand, pupils should write the names of the people that are important to them. Support younger pupils by helping them sound out the names or writing them on a whiteboard to copy.
- Let pupils decorate their hands with coloured pens and pencils.

Lesson plan 2 – Whole class

- This version of the activity is great for when children are new to a classroom or setting, and the result can be displayed for everyone's future reference.

- Draw a large item with five areas that will represent each of the important people. Examples might include a flower with five petals, a crown with five jewels, or a dinosaur with five large spikes.
- Talk to the class about the people that can help them at different times of the day or in different places, for example the class teacher and teaching assistant, a lunch worker, the SENCO, and the headteacher.
- Try to keep it limited to five people, especially if the pupils are new.
- Assign each of the pupils one of the important people.
- Ask your pupils to draw the important people or something to do with their job and how they can help you.
- Pupils could also colour in the main drawing.
- Write the names of the important people in each of the petals, jewels, or spikes.
- Cut out and stick the drawings to the poster, around the name of the person they relate to.

Extensions

Option 1 – Give your pupils some scenarios that they might face and ask them who from their five important people might be able to help them and why they chose that person. These could be realistic or silly situations. For example, you were abducted by aliens and they dyed your hair green, or you are having arguments with a friend at school. This could be extended into a writing activity.

Adaptions

Option 1 – Provide pupils with a list of people that they could include and ask them to choose five to add to their hand. They could copy the names out, trace the letters, or cut out and stick down the provided names.

Stress wheel

When we get stressed, upset, or overwhelmed, it can be difficult to remember how to calm down. This is especially relevant for children, as their emotions can overtake them. This activity gives pupils a chance to think about what helps them regulate and calm down while making a useful tool to be used in the future.

Aims

To consider activities that help you regulate your emotions.

Items needed per group

- Paper plate.
- Coloured pens and pencils.
- Paper clip.
- Straw.
- Scissors.
- Ruler.

Lesson plan – Individuals

- Talk to your class about what feelings can be overwhelming. These could be excitement, anger, sadness, etc.
- When pupils feel these big emotions, what actions might they take that they may regret later, for example hitting a sibling when you're angry, screaming in someone's face when you're excited.
- What could they do to help themselves regulate so they are able to process their thoughts and feelings before acting.
- Each pupil will need a paper plate.
- Using the ruler, draw a line across the centre of the plate in multiple directions to create separate segments. Three lines making six sections works well for this activity.
- In each section, the pupils should write an activity that helps them regulate or calm down.

- They can add drawings and decorations.
- When the decorations are finished, they will need to take a paper clip and open it up fully. Carefully poke a hole in the centre of the paper plate with the paper clip and thread it through halfway.
- Then cut a short piece of the straw (approximately 1 cm). Thread the small piece of the straw onto the paper clip underneath the plate.
- Fold the bottom of the paper clip across the end of the straw to stop it falling off. You should be able to hold the bottom piece with the paper plate balancing on top.
- Cut a longer piece of straw (approximately 5 cm). Thread it onto the paper clip at the top of the plate. Then fold the paper clip over to create a hand like a clock. Don't fold too close to the plate or it won't spin.
- To choose an activity, hold the bottom of the paper clip with one hand and spin the plate with your second hand. When the plate stops, complete the activity the straw hand points to.

Extensions

Option 1 – Each pupil can decorate a cardboard box with a big label stating "[name]'s Regulation Box" or get one box for the class and use the class name. Ask pupils to fill the box with items that would help them regulate and items included on their stress wheels. When pupils are dysregulated or upset, encourage them to go to the Regulation Box to find a tool to help.

Adaptions

Option 1 – Provide pupils with activities that can help them regulate that they can choose from; they can then write or draw an activity in each section of the plate.

Compassion cards

Compassion is noticing someone in need and showing your concern through your actions. This activity gives pupils an opportunity to practice showing compassion in a safe and controlled environment. By acting out and watching different scenarios, pupils can think about the situation and what they might do if it were to happen to them.

Aims

To identify situations that require compassion. To practice acting compassionately towards a peer.

Items needed per group

- Scenario cards.

Lesson plan – Small groups/pairs

- Talk to your class about what compassion is. Compassion is seeing someone in need, caring about their feelings, and then doing something to show that you care.
- Give the pupils some time to suggest times they have shown compassion, or when someone has been compassionate to them.
- Split the class into small groups and give each group a few scenario cards. They will need to choose one card to turn into a scene.
- Working together, each team should take time to prepare a scene enacting the chosen scenario. Each scene will need to show a person who needs compassion and another showing compassion.
- Ask each group to perform their scene to the rest of the class. Ask their peers to think about who in the scene needed compassion, who acted compassionately, and how were they able to tell. And finally, what did acting compassionately do to help the person who needed compassion?

Example scenarios: Someone doesn't understand the rules of a game everyone is playing; someone fell off their scooter and hurt themselves; someone is sitting on their own at lunch time; someone has dropped their snack on the ground and it got trodden on; someone missed the bus to get to school; someone has to go to the doctor for a blood test but is scared of needles; someone has a big test they are worried about; your friend is at your house and wants to play with your favourite toy; your sister/brother is sick; someone's adult has told them they are moving school.

Extensions

Option 1 – Give the pupils longer to prepare their scenes, but ask them to create two versions of the scenario. In the first, the scene starts with the incident, and the person responding is rude or doesn't understand why someone needs compassion. In the second, the person responding shows compassion. Talk about the different responses and how they would make you feel.

Option 2 – Compassion isn't just for other people; we also have to be self-compassionate. Take the scenario cards and ask each group to discuss how a person can be compassionate towards themselves or help themselves in the situation.

Adaptions

Option 1 – Give each group a specific scenario to act out. Support the pupils to come up with some ideas on how to respond to the situation before they practice acting it out.

Kindness calendar

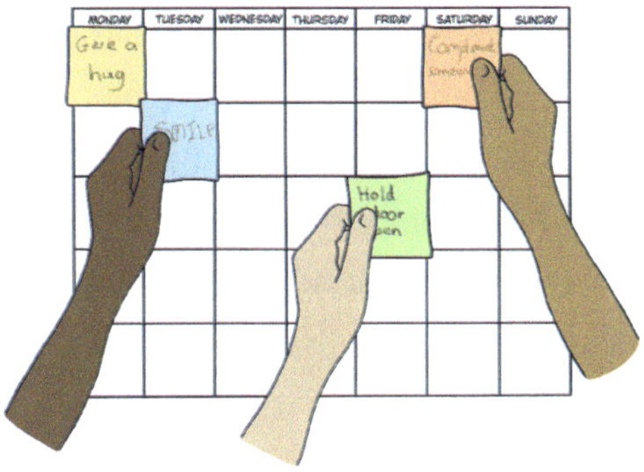

Being kind to others is a great way to improve everyone's mood. A simple action can make someone smile or improve their day. There are lots of ways to be kind, but sometimes we get caught up in our own world and we forget to pass on some happiness.

Aims

To identify ways to show kindness to yourself and to others.

Items needed per group

- Coloured pens/pencils.
- Print out calendar of the next month (1).
- Squares of paper (2).

Lesson plan – Individual

- Each pupil will need a printout calendar for the next month.
- Talk to your class about what it means to be kind. Talk about the things that we can do to make other people feel good and what can we do to make their day better.
- In each box, pupils should write or draw a kind thing that they could do each day. Encourage them to include things that are kind to others and kind to themselves.
- They can also add decorations to their calendar.
- Pupils should try and complete a kind action at some point during each day. They could be kind to their friends, a teacher, parent, or anyone else.

Lesson plan – Whole class

- This activity will create a giant calendar with each pupil making one or two days of it.
- Talk to your class about what it means to be kind. Talk about the things that we can do to make other people feel good and what can we do to make their day better.
- In a place that everyone can see, write the numbers 1–30 or the number of pupils in your class.

- Work with your class to think of something kind that everyone in the class could do, one for every number.
- Allocate a number to each member of the class.
- Give each pupil a square piece of paper.
- They will need to start by writing the number in the top left corner.
- They should then write the kind action on their paper.
- Once the writing is done, let the pupils decorate their square. They could add drawings of the action or just colour and shapes to make it look good.
- When everyone is finished, lay out the pieces of paper like a calendar and tape them together.
- Display the calendar somewhere everyone can see. Each morning, look at the calendar and read out the next number's kind action.
- Pupils should try and complete the kind action at some point during the day. They could be kind to their friends, a teacher, parent, or anyone else.

Examples of kind actions to be included: Pick up some litter; make friends with someone new; hold the door open for someone; write a positive message for someone; give someone a compliment; hold a bake sale for charity; clean up an activity without being asked; smile and say hello to someone; be kind to yourself and do something you love.

Adaption

Option 1 – Provide pupils with kind actions on a sheet of paper that they can cut out and stick to their calendar and then decorate independently.

Reference List

1. Tacikowski, P., Weijs, M.L. and Ehrsson, H.H., 2020. Perception of our own body influences self-concept and self-incoherence impairs episodic memory. *Iscience*, *23*(9), p.101429.

2. Agnafors, S., Barmark, M. and Sydsjö, G., 2021. Mental health and academic performance: A study on selection and causation effects from childhood to early adulthood. *Social Psychiatry and Psychiatric Epidemiology*, *56*, pp.857–866.

3. Bas, G., 2021. Relation between student mental health and academic achievement revisited: A meta-analysis. *Health and academic achievement-new findings*. IntechOpen.

4. Wentzel, K.R., Jablansky, S. and Scalise, N.R., 2021. Peer social acceptance and academic achievement: A meta-analytic study. *Journal of Educational Psychology*, *113*(1), p.157.

5. National Curriculum in England: PE programmes of study. https://www.gov.uk/government/publications/national-curriculum-in-england-physical-education-programmes-of-study; Statutory guidance: Relationships education (Primary). https://www.gov.uk/government/publications/relationships-education-relationships-and-sex-education-rse-and-health-education/relationships-education-primary

* 9 7 8 1 0 3 2 8 4 8 3 3 4 *

T - #0093 - 131224 - C280 - 297/210/13 - PB - 9781032848334 - Gloss Lamination